YOU CAN BE FREE

YOU CAN BE FREE

OVERCOMING TEMPTATION AND
HABITUAL SIN BY THE POWER AND
PROMISES OF THE GOSPEL

KIRBY KELLY

W Publishing Group

An Imprint of Thomas Nelson

Published in Nashville, Tennessee, by W Publishing, an imprint of Thomas Nelson.

Author represented by Trinity McFadden of The Bindery Agency.

Thomas Nelson titles may be purchased in bulk for educational, business, fundraising, or sales promotional use. For information, please email SpecialMarkets@ThomasNelson.com.

Unless otherwise noted, Scripture quotations are taken from the Holy Bible, New International Version®, NIV®. Copyright © 1973, 1978, 1984, 2011 by Biblica, Inc.® Used by permission of Zondervan. All rights reserved worldwide. www.zondervan.com. The "NIV" and "New International Version" are trademarks registered in the United States Patent and Trademark Office by Biblica, Inc.®

Scripture quotations marked CSB are taken from the Christian Standard Bible®. Copyright © 2017 by Holman Bible Publishers. Used by permission. Christian Standard Bible® and CSB® are federally registered trademarks of Holman Bible Publishers.

Scripture quotations marked ESV are taken from the ESV® Bible (The Holy Bible, English Standard Version®). Copyright © 2001 by Crossway, a publishing ministry of Good News Publishers. Used by permission. All rights reserved.

Scripture quotations marked GNT are taken from the Good News Translation in Today's English Version—Second Edition. Copyright © 1992 by American Bible Society. Used by permission.

Scripture quotations marked ISV are taken from the Holy Bible: International Standard Version®. Copyright © 1996–2012 by The ISV Foundation. All right reserved internationally. Used by permission.

Scripture quotations marked LSV are taken from The Holy Bible, Literal Standard Version. Copyright © 2020 by Covenant Press and the Covenant Christian Coalition.

Scripture quotations marked MSG are taken from THE MESSAGE. Copyright © 1993, 2002, 2018 by Eugene H. Peterson. Used by permission of NavPress. All rights reserved. Represented by Tyndale House Publishers, a Division of Tyndale House Ministries.

Scripture quotations marked NKJV are taken from the New King James Version®. Copyright © 1982 by Thomas Nelson. Used by permission. All rights reserved.

Scripture quotations marked NLT are taken from the Holy Bible, New Living Translation. Copyright © 1996, 2004, 2015 by Tyndale House Foundation. Used by permission of Tyndale House Ministries, Carol Stream, Illinois 60188. All rights reserved.

Scripture quotations marked NRSV are taken from the New Revised Standard Version Bible. Copyright © 1989 National Council of the Churches of Christ in the United States of America. Used by permission. All rights reserved worldwide.

Any internet addresses, phone numbers, or company or product information printed in this book are offered as a resource and are not intended in any way to be or to imply an endorsement by Thomas Nelson, nor does Thomas Nelson vouch for the existence, content, or services of these sites, phone numbers, companies, or products beyond the life of this book.

ISBN 978-1-4003-3776-7 (audiobook)
ISBN 978-1-4003-3775-0 (eBook)
ISBN 978-1-4003-3774-3 (softcover)

Library of Congress Control Number: 2023951087

Printed in the United States of America

24 25 26 27 28 LBC 5 4 3 2 1

*Dedicated to my mother, Susan Christine Minnick,
who was my biggest cheerleader, my mama
bear, and the strongest woman I ever knew.
She is forever free in the arms of Jesus, where
pain, suffering, and sin are no more!*

CONTENTS

CONTENTS

FOREWORD

Is there a way for us to *actually* be free?

Not to just declare, "I am free," or to post a pretty and profound quote on social media about feeling free, or to act in such a way that makes others *think* we are free.

I'm talking about when no one else is around. When we are alone with our thoughts. When no one is there to witness our chosen exterior and we are reminded of our very real interior selves. When memories of what we have done, what we said, or what we wish we had done or said start haunting our minds. When we feel weighed down by the shame of something we are not proud of or consumed by guilt for what we wish we were free of.

We might wonder, *Is this all life will ever be?* Will we always feel a little held back? By that one secret kept hidden. By that one story we will never say out loud. By always feeling like we can't ever be our full selves around anyone.

Or . . . can we *actually* be free?

We can.

I used to think freedom was possible for some people but not for me. I grew up witnessing spectacular moments of freedom. My dad battled a heroin addiction for fifteen years, gave his life to Jesus, and completely turned his life around. He started an outreach to those living without homes and battling addiction on the streets of San Francisco, and every month of my childhood I saw men and women throw down their needles, throw away their alcohol bottles, surrender to Jesus, and begin living a completely new life. I witnessed real-life amazing grace. And it was beautiful.

And yet, as I got older, I didn't see this grace as amazing enough for me. I thought it was wonderful for my dad and our friends who were part of these public, profound, and spiritual moments, but it didn't seem realistic for my own life. In the back of my mind I believed I would always be defined by pivotal moments in my past—what was taken from me, what I lost, and what I gave away. How I acted, how I overspoke, what I should've done better, and what I never should have done. The people I hurt, and the ways I hurt myself. Though I have experienced a lot of healing in my life and victory over things I never thought possible, there were some things I resolved could never be healed, labels I would always be defined by, and moments from my past that would always hold me back. I thought I would always be stuck half-living.

I was wrong.

The Word of God reveals a different way to live. A lighter and freer way to live.

I grew up hearing about abundant life, healing for our souls, and freedom from our sins, and yet, for years, I did not know the practical ways to access these things in my own real, everyday life. All the concepts seemed sensational and spiritual but over my head and unattainable.

It took me years to discover what my dear friend Kirby has so graciously and practically laid out in the pages of *You Can Be Free*. She does not sugarcoat the wrong turns we take or the roadblocks we face. Instead, she is courageously honest about living while held back by shame, but also reveals refreshing truths of a real way forward. With tender authority she writes, "You are not a horrible person; you're a human who can be freed from painful patterns and past reputations."

I am living proof that this is true.

When we choose to hold on to our wounds, they become walls that stand in the way of our true healing. But there is another way. There is actual healing in getting real with ourselves, with God, and with other people. There is real freedom in confession. This isn't just available to *some* people. This is available to all of us . . . for you and me, *right now*.

Jesus' brother James instructed us, "Make this your common practice: Confess your sins to each other and pray for each other so that you can live together whole and healed" (James 5:16 MSG).

When we say it out loud—share our sins, our struggles, and our worries with God and with another trusted person—and pray for one another, we will live more healed and more whole. The inverse of that statement is also true. If we do not confess the heaviness welling up inside us, we will live isolated, broken, and disconnected from God and who we really are.

Saying it out loud is our superpower.

Of course, the Enemy of our souls does not want us to get honest with ourselves, with God, or with others. The Enemy knows that he will start to lose his grip when we bring what was hidden into the light.

He wants us to run away from the idea of getting real. He

wants us to see confession, surrender, and obedience as old-school, stuffy, and out-of-date. He wants us to believe the lie that if we told the truth about our life, it would ultimately hurt us, because the Enemy knows that when we bring our hurts, sins, and struggles into the light, we are bringing them into a place where God can come and heal us.

Healing and wholeness are possible . . . *in the light*.

I love the truths Kirby beautifully reveals about confession: "It doesn't blame you, shame you, belittle you, or disqualify you. No, confession is a catalyst that will empower you to be free."

Is there a way to *actually* be free?

There is.

It includes getting real about the problem and getting intentional about the plan. It's not about being strong but about being surrendered. It's not about putting on an impressive show but about taking off the mask and living lighter. It may not be easy, but it is possible.

Let my friend Kirby be your guide to show you how. In the pages of this book, she bravely goes first—she shares real struggles. And then she brilliantly provides tools, outlining practical, doable steps that will help you live freer than you knew was possible.

Take this book as your permission slip to be fully and honestly you.

Take these pages as reminders that you were never meant to live weighed down, held back, or hiding who you really are.

Not only *can* you be free, but you were *created* to live free. As you embrace the freedom available to you, you will start to discover who you really are and step into the life you were created to live.

FOREWORD

If you're ready for a fresh breath, to be set free from guilt and shame, and to be rid of the weights that have held you back, turn the page.

Real, actual freedom is available for you and me, today.

—HOSANNA WONG, international speaker, spoken word artist, and bestselling author of *You Are More Than You've Been Told*

CHAPTER ONE

ALLOW ME TO GO FIRST

Soooooo . . . what's everyone's biggest sin struggle?"

This is the icebreaker I always use when I meet a new group of people. It tickles me to hear the rush of that awkward silence and then the burst of nervous laughter that follows. Christian and non-Christian friends alike can be spooked by the transparency of that question, and I don't blame them. That kind of vulnerability right off the bat isn't all that common for people who have just met. I have yet to get an outright honest answer, but it does eventually lead to everyone meeting each other and having fun and fruitful conversations. Perhaps it's the extrovert in me that gets tickled by this call-and-response. As silly and out of pocket as the question may seem, I genuinely love getting to know new people and cultivating a space where they feel comfortable opening up and forming new connections. I will gladly make a fool of myself

1

to get the conversation flowing and the party going. Ask anyone who knows me!

I start this book with my ridiculous icebreaker because you chose to pick up my book. *This* book. That's right, *I* know the title and subtitle. *I* know what you are about to read, so I have a pretty good idea of your presumptions and hopes about it. You know why? Because this is the book *I* needed when I was in your place and there were no books like this.

Let me begin by expressing how grateful I am that you did pick this book up, because the message, heart, years, and tears that went into it are all a testament to God's glory in my life and what I believe He will do for you. I have walked through seasons and struggles where I just could not seem to get free, and the sin, shame, and defeat were too much to bear. Hopefully my words will bring consolation, confidence, and a loving pinch of conviction for you as you overcome whatever obstacle you're facing and walk out the freedom Christ bought for you.

Whether you know who I am or not, I realize we are still somewhat strangers. Maybe you have a few reservations or worries about what I'm going to say. Perhaps you're thinking:

Who is this girl?

Is she really going to talk about sin despite our comfortable "feel-good gospel" culture?

Who is she to talk about this and call me out?

Is she going to condemn and judge me like other Christians have?

Can we just get a little uncomfortable real quick? Like, right off the bat in the first chapter?

Awesome.

I'm going to kick off this book that's filled with tactics, truth, theology, and practical steps by opening the curtains to let the light in, ripping off the Band-Aid to let the surgery begin, and unlocking the storage closet to let the skeleton out (metaphorically of course). I want to break the ice and talk about the sin that trapped me for well over a decade. I'm talking *years*! Because if I am going to coach, teach, and encourage you through your freedom journey, I know I need to be the first one to start this conversation. That's right, I am about to answer my icebreaker question *for real*.

My Dirty Little Secret

The habitual sin I struggled with for most of my life is pretty taboo in the church's eyes. Culture, on the other hand, tends to celebrate, embrace, and promote this sin as a "no big deal" type of habit. The reality is that my sin nearly destroyed me. It messed with my head and my heart. It made looking at myself in the mirror the next morning unbearable. No wonder I kept it hidden so well for so long.

It is not an easy thing for me to open up and talk about, especially since my nickname all throughout high school was "Holy Water," because I so openly lived for Jesus. Whether or not it was meant as an insult to tease me and mock my commitment to Christ, I took pride in that nickname. Knowing that my peers saw me as a believer who loved them, loved Jesus, and loved sharing the good news of the gospel meant everything to me. I wanted to be set apart, to be that shining example of true Christianity in my public high school. Even online, I felt called to start a YouTube channel when I was fourteen, and over the course of high school I felt convicted by God to start making videos for His name, fame, and glory, not my own. Did I get hate online? You bet. Did I also see people give their lives to Christ through my obedience, despite the comments and backlash? Absolutely. Did I get hate in school for my faith? Yep. Did I also see my classmates experience the love and truth of God fully for the first time through my obedience? 100%. I knew I was called to make Christ known in every space and place where I had a platform, influence, and voice.

But along with the ups of wanting to be a world changer for the gospel at school and online came the downs.

Aside from being made fun of, losing a few friends here and there, facing the public school struggle of separation of church and state, and being misunderstood online with my intentions in sharing the gospel, my biggest obstacle lay *within myself*, in my habitual sin, which I made sure to keep hidden. I believed that if anyone knew I was secretly struggling with a porn addiction and lustful thoughts (yep, we are going there), it would not only ruin my witness but disqualify me from God's love and presence. Now, looking back with an accurate lens of truth, I know that was a lie, but I was new to the faith at the time and really wrestled with this idea. I mean, I had *just* become a Christian the summer before high school. This was all new for me to navigate. I thought that once I was saved, that temptation, desire, and struggle would fade away in Jesus' name.

But it did not.

It stayed.

It grew.

You know what else grew? The shame, self-hatred, and self-condemnation, along with anxiety that if anyone discovered my "dirty little sin," everyone would judge me for my struggle. Some desires and habits were quickly kicked to the curb when Jesus came into the picture, but this one wanted to overstay its welcome, despite my attempts at evicting it. This sin was a squatter, and it was squatting shame and blame all over the place. It felt as if I had no hope of overcoming my inner desires that had conditioned my flesh so comfortably for so long.

The *flesh* is a term that the apostle Paul used all throughout the New Testament to identify the will and desires within us that often go against God's will and way for us. It's that deep-rooted, itching desire to rebel, disobey, and do life on our own terms—to sin, even though we know it isn't good for us.

I was worried that if I didn't get this desire under control, I would let others down and, most importantly, let God down. I didn't want to upset Him or abuse the grace He'd given me. After all, I knew what it meant to obey God and turn away from sin. But just because I knew it didn't mean I was any good at it, especially in this particular area, where my bad habit became my holding cell. I persistently worried that my performance would affect my proximity with the Father. That my stumbling and struggling made God look at me with disgust, wanting nothing to do with me until I got my act together. I felt hopeless, alone, overwhelmed, and exhausted.

Can You Relate?

Maybe you have never struggled with watching things you shouldn't or battling lustful thoughts and actions like I have. Maybe your battle is waking up in the morning and reaching for anything to numb your pain. Maybe it's trying to fill that void in your life with drunken hookups or running back to that toxic ex because you feel lonely. Maybe it's trolling people online and using gossip to boost your own feeling of self-worth. Perhaps it's excessively shopping and lying to your spouse (or to yourself) about how you're stewarding finances. The list of our personal battles could go on and on and on, and we will cover Scripture's take on sin in a moment. But for now, I want to simply start off by saying that I have been on that bus before—the struggle bus. I've been the one driving it, derailing it, and ignoring my GPS, better known as the conviction of the Holy Spirit and God's Word. The end result? Flat tires, falling into pits, and constantly needing roadside assistance to get me back on course. Honestly, I couldn't change a tire to save my life, literally or spiritually. Praise the Lord that I don't need spiritual insurance, because my premiums would be through the roof with my daily mess-ups, intentional or not.

I am grateful to say that my bondage to porn and lust no longer overcomes me. Through the years of victories and losses, by the truth of God's Word and His close presence, I have been able to come out the other side free indeed from the monster that once enslaved me. That sin? It has no hold on me! The shame? Nowhere to be found! Has this temptation tried to trip me up through new tactics in new seasons of life? Absolutely. In this ongoing war, there have been battles I've faced since overcoming my desire to watch porn. The difference, though, is what I know now, and that's what we are about to unpack together: the ongoing battle plan for the war you will wage throughout your life. I know that sounds a bit daunting, but truthfully, you should feel excited! I've faced many battles since those struggles and slayed that same beast over and over again, and you can too. It feels good to win, and that's how I want you to feel.

Knowing the truth about my sin—about the tactics of fighting back in this war against our flesh and our common Enemy's attacks—brought me freedom. Even as I continue to fight, I fight for freedom, from freedom! That's why I can write this book and why I want you to believe me when I say there is hope. You are not alone, and you can be free. I want to show you the way out, because I learned it the hard way myself. It took many years and many tears to get there, but let me save you half the time and tissues in these upcoming pages by helping you sharpen your sword and ready your shield for whatever beast you're facing.

I FIGHT FOR FREEDOM, FROM FREEDOM!

I struggled. I felt defeated. I had wounds that went so deep I thought they would never heal. I felt so alone and was appalled at how I continued to do the things I deeply did not want to do. But look at what God did. Look at what God can do. Look at what God has made available to *you*.

Debt Free by God's Grace

I will be honest with you and tell you that I still face temptation to this day. Shocker, right? It's not like I'm human or anything and that Satan isn't always prowling around looking to devour anything that has a heartbeat (1 Peter 5:8). So even as I write this book, I am applying everything in its contents to my own life, and will continue to do so, because this is a daily battle we're fighting. Temptation and sin may look different from season to season, but we encounter many battles warring against them nonetheless. That doesn't have to be a scary truth or exhausting fact, because

God is with you, and this book will give you practical ways to wage war against the accuser whenever those battles begin.

Friend, you and I are human, and whether you want to overcome sin that has controlled you for decades or prepare for temptations that will cross your path even after finishing this book, I am believing and praying this book will help, heal, equip, and empower you in the truth of the gospel and the authority God has given you as His child. Like Romans 6:18 says, "Having been freed from sin, you became servants to righteousness" (LSV). In Christ, we go from slavery to servanthood, bondage to blessing, stuck to set free. When Jesus died on the cross for our sins, there was a beautiful exchange that took place. He took on our sins, our mistakes, and our wrong decisions, and paid off that debt for us. If you thought student loans were scary, then you don't even want to know how much debt we've acquired in the "don't do that" charges we've accumulated. But Jesus paid it all off and exchanged it for His righteousness, meaning that when God looks at the receipt, He sees *Paid in full*. It's better than a 720 credit score, friend!

IN CHRIST, WE GO FROM SLAVERY TO SERVANTHOOD, BONDAGE TO BLESSING, STUCK TO SET FREE.

When we place our faith in what Jesus did and receive Him as our Savior, Leader, and King, committing to walk in His ways, we can stand before God free! In addition to that, from a place of righteousness (right standing with God), we get to stare down the Enemy and fight *from* victory, *for* victory. We press on from a place of grace. We overcome because Christ overcame. Hear the good news, hold on to it tightly, and get ready to break free!

CHAPTER TWO

STAND FOR YOUR SISTER

I was first exposed to pornography at age four, when I walked in on someone watching it on TV. A few years later, at age seven, I found someone's secret stash of pornographic magazines. Then, at age ten, I was invited to a sleepover where one of my classmates showed me the porn website her brother had exposed her to. Again and again, I was involuntarily subjected to these images, which sadly sparked my curiosity, only to later develop into an uncontrollable, habitual sin cycle of shamefully and secretly watching pornography.

No child should be exposed to porn. Frankly, no adult should either. But statistics show that the majority of young people are exposed to porn by the time they are fourteen. Recent studies have also shown that over 84 percent of fourteen-to-eighteen-year-old males and 57 percent of fourteen-to-eighteen-year-old females have viewed pornography.[1] 28 percent of adolescents who have viewed porn were first exposed by accident; 19 percent were unexpectedly shown pornography by someone else; and only 19 percent first searched for it intentionally.[2] This is a pervasive epidemic that has warped and distorted the minds of youth in regard to safe, loving, consensual, and biblical principles surrounding sex. I, unfortunately, was one of them.

Not only did it tamper with my understanding of sex and intimacy, but that early exposure to porn became an integral part of my life that I couldn't seem to break free from. Four-year-old, seven-year-old, and ten-year-old Kirby should never have been exposed to such explicit and inappropriate content. Nobody of any age should be, whether you're four, fourteen, forty, or four hundred! It disrupts, disturbs, deceives, destroys, and divides as any other sin does.

The struggle was real. *My* struggle was real. For so long I suffered hopelessly in the dark with this habit. Even though this book centers around freedom from sin, the truth is, I debated whether to share this part of my life with you. Everyone knew me as the "purity girl" growing up. When I got saved at the age of fourteen, I asked my mom for a purity ring for Christmas. I mean, who would suspect that the girl who wanted a purity ring for Christmas was struggling with a porn addiction?

I wrestled with this secret sin in silence for years because the stigma and shame around it made me feel isolated, disgusting, and freakish. I mean, this was a "boy's sin," right? That was the popular narrative at least. It seemed to me that girls typically struggled with eating disorders or gossip; meanwhile, I was struggling with X-rated content. All throughout high school, I battled with this temptation in secret, afraid to admit it to anyone because I didn't want to face judgment. I would break free from watching it for a while, then suddenly fall back into the cycle. I would do good for another few weeks, maybe even a few months, then slip right back into it again. Why couldn't I get free? I mean, I knew Jesus. I loved Jesus. I was saved by my faith in Jesus and His work on the cross. Why was I still stuck? I felt like Sisyphus from Greek mythology, who repeatedly rolled a giant boulder up a hill only to have it roll back down every time it neared the summit. I was exhausted, and I felt completely alone in my struggle—that is, until I opened up.

Going into my freshman year at Dallas Baptist University (DBU), I knew I had to truly face and overcome this habitual sin. Enough was enough. I wanted it gone. I needed a fresh start and freedom. A few months into that first semester, I joined a Christian sorority called Sigma Chi Eta (whoop, whoop!), and I embarked on a camping retreat as a first bonding experience with both returning members and fellow new members.

We drove all the way up to middle-of-nowhere Oklahoma and pitched a bunch of tents by a river. We explored the wildlife and outdoors, played games at the campsite, roasted hot dogs and s'mores, sang songs, and shared hilarious stories as we got to know one another. Seriously, I think I laughed so hard I peed my pants— those girls were too funny. Who doesn't love a community like that? After all the fun and games, our president handed out a sheet of paper to each girl that read "Stand for Your Sister" at the top.

Glancing down my page, I surveyed the anonymous poll we all had to fill out, including statements like these:

- I struggle with an eating disorder: True or False
- I come from a divorced family: True or False

- I often feel like an outcast/forgotten about: True or False
- I am ashamed of my past and cannot forgive myself for it: True or False
- I have been a victim of bullying: True or False
- I struggle with watching pornography: True or False

Those were just a few of the many questions we answered anonymously. I'm sure you and your friends could add so many things to this list based on your own experiences:

- I can't stop self-harming: True or False
- I lie to make people like me: True or False
- I am struggling with addiction: True or False
- I use sex or food to numb my anxiety: True or False
- I had an abortion and I regret it: True or False
- I act one way at church and another way with friends: True or False

After filling out our papers, we crumpled them up, threw them at one another, and each unraveled someone else's anonymous answers. With all of us sitting around the campfire, the sorority president encouraged us by saying, "Stand for your sister if they struggle with insecurity." I looked down at the piece of paper I had picked up. One of my sisters had circled *True* on it. Of the sixty-plus girls there, dozens of us stood. The president directed us to sit, then read off, "Stand for your sister if they use alcohol as a way of escape." Again, several people stood. We went through the entire list. I would stand up and sit down with my sisters to my left and right for similar experiences, including sexual assault, anxiety, depression, and toxic comparison. The president then read, "I struggle with watching pornography." Nervously, I waited for just one person to stand, representing me, but when I looked down at the piece of paper I held, I saw my girl had circled *True*. I stood for her. Then, one by one, nearly half of the girls stood up to represent their sorority sisters who also struggled with the very sin ensnaring me.

Looking around in disbelief, I was shocked at how *not* alone I was in my struggle. All this time, I had been convinced nobody understood the sin and shame I wrestled with.

I WAS SHOCKED AT HOW *NOT* ALONE I WAS IN MY STRUGGLE.

We moved through a couple more prompts, and by the end of our time, many of us were in tears. Our president stood and told us there were more of us than we thought who felt alone or trapped by sins, lies, and past mistakes. She encouraged us to pray for one another and be vulnerable in that community with someone we trusted, because the Enemy wanted us alone and ashamed in our sin. God, on the other hand, has called us to find freedom from sin in community. Truth be told, I didn't confess my struggle with pornography to anyone that night. I was too afraid. I was still ashamed. I wasn't ready right then and there to bare my soul. But as I began to develop a friendship with an older, wiser sorority sister who openly spoke about her past struggles with porn, I knew I had to reach out to her and confess the habitual sin I desperately wanted freedom from.

Not long after the camping trip, I called her up and visited her apartment to share the burden on my heart. As I sat on her couch, the tears quickly welled up and poured out as I finally confessed my sin out loud: "I can't break free from my struggle against pornography. I feel so hopeless, so alone. I just want to be free, and after the camping trip, I knew I needed to confess it to someone."

I explained how it had developed from early childhood exposure into curiosity, temptation, then habitual sin throughout my life. In my heart, I honestly and genuinely wanted to stop, but I hated myself because I simply couldn't tame the desire within me. My flesh craved instant gratification, but my spirit desired to love and please God. My flesh craved old, comfortable habits, but my spirit desired freedom and new life.

With grace and compassion I could only equate with the love of Jesus, she hugged me, assured me, and affirmed me, relating how proud she was that I had confessed my sin and brought it into the light. She shared with me her personal journey with overcoming that cycle of habitual sin, encouraged me with some scriptures, and told me to look up the dark truth behind the porn industry and its harmful effects on its consumers and producers. She reassured me of my trust in the Lord and increased my awareness of sin's strikes in my day-to-day life.

I confessed that sin to a sister who I knew cared for me, understood me, and would encourage me rather than tear me down. So much relief comes when we release what we've kept hidden. It's taxing and exhausting to bottle all that stuff up; we were never meant to carry that kind of burden. It reminds me of that classic trope on TV and in movies where someone cleans up their apartment sporadically and shoves their trash into a closet when someone arrives without notice. They don't want anybody to see the real condition they live in. They hide the mess. They simply move it somewhere else for a while until everyone goes home. Inevitably, someone opens the closet, and it all falls out in the open for everyone to see. For the individuals

SO MUCH RELIEF COMES WHEN WE RELEASE WHAT WE'VE KEPT HIDDEN.

STAND FOR YOUR SISTER

hiding something, it doesn't quite feel like a release. It feels like exposure. Nobody likes their mess to be put on display.

Whether you want to release what has been hidden or your mess has already been exposed, know that there *are* people who won't judge you for what's locked in that closet. Odds are, they, too, have had a closet full of sin struggles they hoped wouldn't see the light of day. But when you bring sin into the light by releasing it (or even having it released through accidental exposure), a loving and trusted community can come alongside you to help sort through the mess, so you can have a safe, clean, and functional space you're happier living in. One where you can freely move about life. I experienced that with my sorority sister—a release that eventually led to freedom.

Surrounded, Supported, and Saved

I am so grateful to say that was the beginning of my journey to freedom. But it didn't happen because I was some kind of super-Christian. Like I said, I had always hoped for freedom from my porn habit, but I couldn't imagine that as a possibility, even in a million years. It was a habit that had been going on for more than half my life. Looking back, I now know that's because I was relying on my own ability, my own strength, and my own reasoning to free me, when I desperately needed a *Savior*. I needed *saving*. Not only that, the Enemy used shame and guilt to isolate me from ever seeking help, prayer, accountability, or any understanding of the psychology of addiction—all necessary to walk in freedom. I never realized how vital it was to actually tell someone else about my struggle in order to kick-start my freedom journey. It's no wonder the Enemy never wanted me to do it; he knows the power and importance of community in making progress and seeing real change in our desires and decisions. That is so like Satan, to gate-keep from us the very ways that lead to freedom. He doesn't want us to find good, godly community to walk alongside us, encourage us, and help us get free. He wants us to remain alone, ashamed, and afraid, and to stuff even more secrets into the hidden parts of our heart until it breaks. He wants to keep God's image-bearers from ever entering the light, because in the light darkness has to flee.

I can't stress this enough: the trusted community surrounding me played a major role in my freedom journey from the sin I believed I could never leave. Confessing and confiding in other women who had struggled like me and understood the compassion and freeing power of Christ were key to shifting my beliefs. I realized that I really could be free.

Do you have anyone or any group of people in your life who knows the Word of God, walks with Jesus daily, and walks out freedom in their own life? Someone who loves you and could serve as a trusted confidant? If the answer is yes, you've taken step one on your journey. Stick with them, and find an opportunity to tell them about your struggles—not to shame, belittle, or expose you in any way that negates your worth or your efforts at improving, but to protect you and to help push back the lies you are believing about yourself. They should surround you, support you, encourage you, equip you, and help you to break free from that area of sin.

If you don't have those people in your life, start praying for God to bring them. Even one person in your corner to support you in moments of weakness or cheer you on in your breakthroughs can create a strong wind under your wings to soar to where God has called you. I had to intentionally find community in college, outside of college, and even as a married woman. I needed and still need women to surround and support me in every season of life, and all the different sins and struggles that come with it. We are created for relationship, and Scripture encourages us to find people to walk with us through life.

WHEN WE CONCEAL RATHER THAN CONFESS, WE END UP BEING A ROADBLOCK TO GOD'S MERCY.

I remember coming across Proverbs 28:13 during this period of my life. It wisely advises believers that "whoever conceals their sins does not prosper, but the one who confesses and renounces them finds mercy." When we conceal rather than confess, we end up being a roadblock to God's mercy. Hiding has been the human response to sin since the beginning. We sin, then we hide. We mess up, then we conceal. I'm going to walk you through all the steps that helped me break free, but first I want you to know that even if you don't have a single person you feel safe telling, you've got me, you've got God, and you've got His Word.

The Angry Guy in the Sky

The Bible is not a book of rules detached from relevancy or reality; it's the story of God and our relationship with Him. It's the guidebook to living life as it was always meant to be lived. It's raw, it's real, it's unfiltered, and it's truth. How cool is that—that God gave us this tool, this road map to wisdom, connection, and freedom? Contrary to our culture's perception, the Bible is not about good mantras and fairy-tale bedtime stories. It is historically true, spiritually true, and it affects our day-to-day lives. God is not some far-off angry guy in the sky striking us with lightning every time we do something wrong. No, He is near, He is close, He is involved, and He wants to do life with us. He loves us despite all the mess—so much that He made a way to alleviate that mountain of regret that piles up on us and that heap of shame that topples onto us. If we are to understand our sin (aka the things we keep doing that hurt us, yet we still can't seem to stop), then we have to allow the Bible to be our guide and speak into our lives. To start getting free we have to go back to the beginning, when sin first entered the world.

Where Are You Hiding?

Before we talk about anything else, let's focus on what happened after Adam and Eve sinned. Moments after their biggest flop, their most tragic failure, their gravest mistake, *God came looking for His beloved kids.* Where were they? They were hiding, just like I hid for years in my own sin. But God loved them so much (and loves us the same) that He called out to them. "Then the man and his wife heard the sound of the LORD God as he was walking in the garden in the cool of the day, and they hid from the LORD God among the trees of the garden. *But the LORD God called to the man,* 'Where are you?' He answered, 'I heard you in the garden, and I was afraid because I was naked; so I hid'" (Genesis 3:8–10, emphasis added). Out of their shame, out of their vulnerability exposed by their sin, out of fear, Adam and Eve hid from God. But God did not abandon them in that moment. He called out to them, wanting them in His presence, not in isolation or separation.

God's first question in the entire Bible, directed to Adam and Eve, was, *Where are you?* Contrary to what we often think about God, He doesn't hide His face or turn His back on us in the face of our sin, shame, and exposure. Friend, He does the exact opposite. God comes looking for us. *We* are the ones who hide, run away, and try to cover up with fig leaves like Adam and Eve. He asks, *My beloved child, where are you?* because He wants us to be in His presence. In intimacy, not isolation. He wants us to remember the truth that He always seeks us out, chasing after us even when we feel the least desirable or worthy. In every moment of every day, God is looking out for us and desires to be near us, even when we fall into sinful situations and give in to temptation. He doesn't run up to us and say, *Hey, I saw that! How dare you! Right in front of Me?* No, He says, *Where are you hiding? Come to Me. I want to help make your wrong right by covering you and cleansing you with My sacrifice.*

Never forget the lengths God traveled to pay for your sins with the sacrifice of Jesus. He gave His life so we could live a real, truly free life, cleansed from our sin by the covering of His assurance and total forgiveness. Hear me loud and clear: He would go to any length to find, rescue, and redeem you because of His

GOD DOES NOT WANT YOU TO HIDE YOUR MISTAKES AND MESS; HE WANTS YOU TO COME TO HIM SO HE CAN HEAL THE HURT.

perfect love for you. He doesn't love or not love us based on what we've done. He simply loves us. *He* loves you. He *loves* you. He loves *you!*

God does not want you to hide your mistakes and mess; He wants you to come to Him so He can heal the hurt. He is near, standing in the light. For He is the light, and that is where He calls us to meet Him. "But if we walk in the light, as he is in the light, we have fellowship with one another, and the blood of Jesus, his Son, purifies us from all sin" (1 John 1:7). In the light, He cleanses, purifies, and covers the places we have fallen short. This is a promise. This is the truth. Only in the light can we truly see our sin for what it is and receive healing from its hurt and harm in our life. Like mold, sin thrives in the darkness, its toxic spores killing us with every breath. But in the light, God can mold us into who He called and created us to be. He has a bigger and more beautiful future for you than you could even imagine.

The fact is, we will always struggle with sin. First John 1:8 says, "If we claim to be without sin, we deceive ourselves and the truth is not in us." But here is the amazing reality: "If anyone does sin, we have an advocate with the Father—Jesus Christ, the Righteous One" (1 John 2:1). Friend, did you get that? *Jesus Himself stands for you.*

Jesus. Stands. For. You.

He is our advocate, our representative. He knows what is written on your most secret list. And He stands in place of you. He meets your sins with mercy, and

JESUS KNOWS WHAT IS WRITTEN ON YOUR MOST SECRET LIST. AND HE STANDS IN PLACE OF YOU.

He never gives up on you. He never stops looking for you. He is the road to freedom from your sins. I know it to be true in my own life. Am I still tempted? Yes. Do I sin in other ways? Yes. But I have made a habit of surrounding myself with a community who has permission to be real with me and ask the hard questions, to

STAND FOR YOUR SISTER

pray for me and encourage me in truth. They cultivate a space where confession is not met with judgment but with the goal of moving forward in freedom. That has given me hope and allowed me to experience the joys and promises of deliverance from my old desires. If it's been true for me through the truth of His Word, you can have that same hope and expectancy in your life too. Jesus stands with you and for you, and I stand with you and for you, too, friend. I want you to be free. I believe you can be free. Let's keep learning the steps together.

Connect and Confess

Let's recap everything we just discussed and the action steps you can take in your freedom journey:

- Acknowledge your sin and its reign and ruin in your life.
- Seek out a healthy and trustworthy community of believers through prayer and get connected with them.
- Cultivate authentic relationships and share your secret sin. Bring it into the light to clearly see it and position yourself for healing.
- Ask for accountability in turning away from this sin. Devise healthy ways to communicate with your safe people in times of weakness so they can pray for you, encourage you, and call you off the path of destruction.

CHAPTER THREE

OUT OF BOUNDS

One night while I was serving with the youth group at my church, a guest speaker spoke with us about boundaries. She explained how they are important and amazing because they provide protection, peace, and freedom. Contrary to popular opinion, we can actually move *freely* within boundaries; they are not constricting! I can move freely around a soccer field as I kick the ball, but the lines around the field mark the space that constitutes "out of bounds." I can paddleboard around an inlet safely as long as boats obey the signs indicating a No Wake Zone. If the boaters drive above the proper speed limit, it would compromise my safety and theirs. When driving down the interstate, the lines on the road indicate separate lanes to ensure everyone's safety. Swerving may cause you to damage your car or even put yourself or someone else in danger. Those boundary lines provide safety and the best possible direct route to get you where you need to go.

The Holy Spirit acts as our GPS, guiding us along the route

to get to where He has called us. Sometimes, though, we veer to the left, to the right, or take an exit before He instructs us to, and we end up at the wrong location. Have you ever ended up on the wrong side of town because you cut corners and took a few turns way too soon? The truth is, we can get lost if we don't listen to that GPS, especially if we are in unfamiliar territory. But similar to a GPS, God also reroutes us to His intended destination: where He has prepared a place for us. Maybe there are a few more potholes we encounter or red lights and stop signs that require patience. Maybe we even end up in a ditch some days because of our dang detours, but He will get us back on that road if we choose to listen and obey His directions. They'll lead us to our destination. And do you know what you are destined for as a child of God? Protection, peace, and *freedom*.

Boundaries, commands, rules, and guidelines can seem restrictive because of what the world views as acceptable and because of the desires of our flesh. However, boundaries actually create the safest and most life-giving places, whether you're swimming in the ocean or navigating your life safely away from sin. It was true in the garden before the fall, and it is true for us today, wherever you are in life. God clearly communicated and set boundaries back in Genesis 2:16–17: "And the LORD God commanded the man, saying, 'You may surely eat of every tree of the garden, but of the tree of the knowledge of good and evil you shall not eat, for in the day that you eat of it you shall surely die'" (ESV). If God established the need for boundaries from the very beginning to prevent sin and make a way for a close and life-giving relationship with Him, how much more necessary are boundaries for us today as Christians who face the opposition of temptation to sin daily?

Did God Really Say . . .

The Bible contains our origin story. Adam and Eve did not just eat a piece of fruit, and then the world went crazy. They were influenced by the voice, the lies, and the twisted truth fed to them by the Serpent. That led to the consequence of separation between them and God. Genesis 3:1 says, "Now the serpent was more crafty than any of the wild animals the LORD God had made. He said to the woman, 'Did God really say, "You must not eat from any tree in the garden"?'" In case you were not aware, the Serpent was Satan (Revelation 12:9). Knowing full well God's stipulations and boundaries for Adam and Eve, Satan came to them and questioned what God had said to them. He called into question God's order, authority, and voice when he asked them, "Did God really say . . . ?" Eve replied with a paraphrase of God's instructions, that if they ate of the Tree of Knowledge of Good and Evil, she and Adam would die. The Serpent responded cunningly, "You will not certainly die. . . . For God knows that when you eat from it your eyes will be opened, and *you* will be *like God*, knowing good and evil" (vv. 4–5, emphasis added).

Three major things are true about our identity. First, if you are human, you are made in God's image. Every person bears God's image, whether you believe in Him or not, whether you're saved or unsaved. We display His glory and existence through our own existence.

Second, we can do nothing to earn the title and essence of an image-bearer. We do not *perform* for this role; we simply *are* image-bearers. God interweaves it in everyone's DNA from the moment they are conceived, giving each person dignity,

BEING GOD'S IMAGE-BEARER IS THE MOST FUNDAMENTAL PART OF EVERY PERSON'S IDENTITY.

individuality, and worth. Being God's image-bearer is the most fundamental part of every person's identity.

Third, our identity as image-bearers enables us to fulfill our calling, act upon our own free will, reason and reflect, and interact with others and God.

Let's consider that for a moment. Isn't it interesting what the Enemy chose to attack? First, *God's voice*, and second, *our identity*. He influenced Eve and her husband, Adam, to misinterpret God's voice and eat the fruit so they could be like God, when they were *already* made in His likeness, bearing His image. This is *exactly* how Satan works. He distorts, he deceives, and he lies, all in order to trip you and trap you. We need to be aware of his tactics and how he wants to derail us—sending us out of bounds.

Listen = Obey

One of my favorite Hebrew words in the entire Bible is *Shema*. It shows up most notably in Deuteronomy 6:4–9 in a section known as the Shema prayer:

> Hear, O Israel: The LORD our God, the LORD is one. You shall love the LORD your God with all your heart and with all your soul and with all your might. And these words that I command you today shall be on your heart. You shall teach them diligently to your children, and shall talk of them when you sit in your house, and when you

walk by the way, and when you lie down, and when you rise. You shall bind them as a sign on your hand, and they shall be as frontlets between your eyes. You shall write them on the doorposts of your house and on your gates. (ESV)

That first word in Deuteronomy 6:4, *hear*, is *Shema* in Hebrew. But if we know anything about this language, we know these words mean more than our plain English translation. *Shema* does not simply mean "hear"; it more accurately translates as "to listen and obey." Like the Israelites, who were God's chosen people, we who have been adopted into the kingdom of God because of our faith in Jesus are also called to *listen and obey*.

When it comes to the commands, boundaries, and instructions given to us by God, our response should be *Shema*—listening to what He says with the intended response of obedience. So many people claim they want to hear from God, yet they refuse to obey His guidance and instruction. At one point, I *was* this person. I vividly remember being in an insanely dark season of life where I allowed my own desires to triumph over the commands and boundaries God gave me. I did what I wanted and used God's grace as a cop-out. I told myself, *He'll forgive me later anyway, so what's the big deal, right?* Wrong. Deep down, my heart was severely suffering from living in darkness and disobedience disguised as liberation and freedom. That was not true freedom but true foolishness.

What I suffered from most in that season was *silence*. I kept asking God why I wasn't hearing from Him, but the answer was quite clear: God hadn't stopped speaking; I had stopped listening and obeying. My disobedient decisions and desires did all they could to muffle the sweet whisper of God in my life. My sinfulness and willingness to please my every whim kept me from clearly and confidently hearing from God and obeying His words. I am so grateful that before I continued down a more destructive path, I realized this, genuinely repented (turned from my sin), and began living my life in step with Christ. Not only was it far better to be back in bounds, but His voice became clearer once my own chatter started to cease. I grew to realize that God actually was speaking that entire time by calling me out of my sin, back into His loving and protective arms. He didn't want me getting hurt, suffering from a broken heart, and making decisions I'd live to regret. He continually called me back to closeness with Him, to step where He led so I would be filled with joy, peace, and purpose.

GOD IS LOVING, GRACIOUS, AND MERCIFUL. HE STILL SPEAKS TO US, EVEN WHEN WE REFUSE TO LISTEN PROPERLY AND RESPOND IN OBEDIENCE.

God is loving, gracious, and merciful. He still speaks to us, even when we refuse to listen properly and respond in obedience. He directs us back to Him, because it's on that path of obedience that we can hear God distinctly, stay in bounds, and live free.

Love Him with Everything

Let's revisit the Shema prayer for a second. Jesus later repeated this command in Mark 12:30 and called it the greatest commandment! He worded it like this: "'And you shall love the LORD your God with all your heart, with all your soul, with all your mind, and with all your strength.' This is the first commandment" (NKJV).

We are to love God with all our *heart*: with all our emotions and feelings.

We are to love God with all our *soul*: with all our desires and will.

We are to love God with all our *mind*: with all our reasoning and consideration.

We are to love God with all our *strength*: with all our ability and diligence.

Friend, God doesn't want just your good works, your perfect record, or your A+ performance. He wants your *love*! It makes my heart melt that, above all else, God desires a relationship with us built on the premise of love. Sit with that for a minute and think about all the things we so often imagine God expects from us. Oftentimes, we're the ones who place the burden of unrealistic expectations on our shoulders, not God. Ultimately, He wants us to simply love Him with every ounce of our being, because out of that love comes an overflow of devotion, desire, obedience, and understanding. It is by love, out of love, from love, and in love we trust and obey His will and way.

> FRIEND, GOD DOESN'T WANT JUST YOUR GOOD WORKS, YOUR PERFECT RECORD, OR YOUR A+ PERFORMANCE. HE WANTS YOUR *LOVE*!

Simply put, "We love because he first loved us" (1 John 4:19). We have this ability and opportunity to love the God of the universe because He went to every extent to display His love for us, even to the point of Jesus willingly dying on the cross so nothing would separate us from Him. Because of Jesus' sacrifice, we are now able to walk with

Him freely, without the stain or strain of sin, us in Him and He in us. We are God's dwelling place, and if we choose Him, He will make His home in our hearts. He is closer to you than you think!

But what does God's love look like? How do we properly love Him? I had this major question when I first gave my life to Jesus. I wanted to know and honor God, but above all else, I wanted to love Him in the ways He wanted to be loved, not simply with the love we see in this world—a love that is often received and reciprocated out of merit and with conditions. I wanted to love God as He loved me: unconditionally, faithfully, fully, and attentively.

Jesus put it plainly in John 14:15. "If you love me, keep my commands."

Jesus feels loved when we do what He says? *Yes.* But you see, it's not because He's all about rule-following. No, our obedience communicates that we trust and believe that His ways are better because *He* is better than any other person or path we could chase. First Samuel 15:22 says, "And Samuel said, 'Has the LORD as great delight in burnt offerings and sacrifices, as in obeying the voice of the LORD? Behold, to obey is better than sacrifice, and to listen than the fat of rams'" (ESV). God desires for us to *listen* and *obey*. That displays our love and trust toward Him, our sacrifice to Him, because we offer up control of our life to Him. We call Him the *Lord* over our lives, who reigns out of His love for us. The heart that listens to and obeys God reflects an unwavering love for Him, devotion to His will, and obedience toward His good plans for them.

> OUR OBEDIENCE COMMUNICATES THAT WE TRUST AND BELIEVE THAT HIS WAYS ARE BETTER BECAUSE *HE* IS BETTER THAN ANY OTHER PERSON OR PATH WE COULD CHASE.

Whenever God has asked me to surrender something to Him and trust in His control, whatever waited for me on the other side was always better. If I had pursued my original dream of acting instead of submitting my purpose and vocation to God, I never would have found the joy of creating content in ministry. If I had pursued relationships God told me to surrender, I never would have met my husband—my perfect person. If I had pursued attending the university I originally committed to and passed up the Holy Spirit's conviction to switch to DBU, I never would have discovered my gifts and talents, or had the opportunities and community that I found there. So many dreams and desires, and so much growth were the result of my obedience!

FRIEND, I DON'T KNOW WHAT GOD IS TELLING YOU TO LET GO OF TODAY, BUT LAY THAT THING DOWN.

Friend, I don't know what God is telling you to let go of today, but lay that thing down. Listen and obey His voice! I wholeheartedly believe that if you have your hands on this book, you want freedom from your sin and so desperately want to be close to God and live out His plans for your life. So surrender what He requires of you, because what He gives you in exchange will be far better than whatever you're clinging to for hope, comfort, security, or direction.

Where Do I Even Start?

Perhaps you've read up until this point, and all this knowledge has drawn out a few "Ooh, that's good" responses from you. However, you're still wanting more. More practicals. More tactics.

More how-tos. More ways to break through what has been breaking you. Sin is no joke, especially habitual sin. Temptation is no joke either. But in order to move forward in faith, freedom, and fullness of life, we first have to take a necessary step back.

My mom's favorite movie was *The Wizard of Oz*. In the movie, Dorothy and her hodgepodge of hay-stuffed, tin-coated, and whiskered friends journey across the land of Oz on the yellow brick road to find what they seek. When they finally reach the Emerald City to visit the great and powerful Oz, they come face-to-face with a fearful beast of a man—only to have the illusion destroyed by a tiny terrier. Dorothy and her crew discover a man hidden behind a curtain, pulling all sorts of bells and whistles, operating the illusion of a so-called Wizard of Oz. He has no real power; the illusion is shattered. I want to do that for us in the next chapter with the grand illusionist many of us fear: our enemy, Satan.

IF YOU WANT TO BREAK DOWN THE STRONGHOLDS OF SIN IN YOUR LIFE AND BREAK THROUGH THOSE PRISONLIKE CHAINS VICTORIOUSLY, YOU NEED TO RECOGNIZE THE ENEMY'S NATURE, TACTICS, AND MOTIVES FOR SCHEMING AGAINST YOU.

I know it doesn't seem fun to talk about sin and Satan, but the only way to defeat your enemy is to know him. We need to pull back the curtain and see what kind of levers he's pulling and schemes he's devising against you. I love how Sun Tzu phrased this idea in the ancient work *The Art of War*: "If you know the enemy and know yourself, you need not fear the result of a hundred battles. If you know yourself but not the enemy, for every victory gained you will also suffer a defeat.

If you know neither the enemy nor yourself, you will succumb in every battle."[1] Friend, if you want to break down the strongholds of sin in your life and break through those prisonlike chains victoriously, you need to recognize the Enemy's nature, tactics, and motives for scheming against you. He has taken too much territory in your life. He has overstayed his welcome with his pestering, luring, and condemning. He has taken captive too much of your heart, soul, mind, and strength. To him I say, "Oh, it's on!" It's not just time for war but spiritual warfare. Let's suit up for the battlefield, together.

BATTLE PLAN STEP #2:
Stay in Bounds

Before launching into our battle plan, I want to summarize some key truths as a foundation for our faith journey:

- God lays out boundaries not to restrict us or take away the fun in life. Biblical boundaries unlock the fullness of life God has for us in Christ and provide for us peace, protection, and freedom from sin and temptation.
- The Enemy will do everything he can to deceive us about God's identity and our own, and use that to divide us from God's peace, protection, and freedom. Satan wants to steer us off God's path into rebellion, lawlessness, and darkness. Fortunately, God is faithful, forgiving, and fully willing to redeem us and help us get back on the road toward the dreams and destiny He has for us.
- *Shema* means "to listen and obey," and that is how we greatly love God. We reciprocate His love by loving Him through our actions of trust, obedience, surrender, and faith.
- The Lord loves us far greater than anyone or anything ever could, and He proved this by giving up His own life to spare ours from sin and death.

CHAPTER FOUR

EXPOSING
THE ENEMY

When you think of the devil, what imagery pops into your mind? Perhaps it's a little red guy with a pitchfork, horns, and a pointed tail. Where is he hanging out? In an underground cave with lava lakes and flames, or chilling on your left shoulder? We've all seen him portrayed as cheeky, funny, reasonable, wicked, logical, and even willing to work with people.

He's also been portrayed as a friendly, devilish peer of sorts, with hell as just a big party he's throwing. I mean, if he's the one who approves all the "fun things" that God doesn't, wouldn't you rather chill with that guy? Some flat-out deny that hell and Satan even exist, while others have created religions to literally worship Satan, convinced he is the foundation for intellect, free will, and reasoning—things God must oppose since the devil represents them, *right*?

I hope my sarcasm came through quite clearly. These contrived stories, assumptions, and caricatures of Satan are just that: false. The Enemy is cunning and crafty at portraying himself as a naughty friend, a sexy intellectual symbol, and even straight-up nonexistent. I mean, if someone sees him as their best buddy, why would they even give Jesus a chance? Or if someone thinks he is obsolete, where is the worry and need for a Savior? If you can get people on your good side or, better yet, to think you're a myth, you can slip through the cracks and really get down to business stealing, killing, and destroying them (John 10:10).

It reminds me of the horror movie *The Invisible Man*. He was the worst kind of intruder because he could stalk and terrorize his girlfriend with impunity because no one believed he was real. That is the mission and motive of the devil. But do you know what the Bible compares the devil to? How God described this supposed cartoon character? "Your adversary the devil is prowling around like a roaring lion, looking for anyone he can devour" (1 Peter 5:8 CSB). Yes, the creature we either ignore or make fun of is literally stalking us right now. And God wants us to be prepared.

Satan in the Spotlight

These false narratives we believe about the devil make me think of the musical *Pippin*, one of my favorite Broadway shows. Get ready for some spoilers. In the musical, you have Pippin, a young prince who represents the normal man seeking his purpose and place in life. Everything takes place in a circus-like setting where the Leading Player and performance troupe set up scenes as Pippin moves through some of life's most defining moments. Under his father's rule as king, Pippin tries to find significance as a combat soldier in war, in religion, in meaningless relationships, in helping the poor, and in genuine love and family. Meanwhile, all throughout Pippin's journey of self-discovery, the Leading Player who is conducting this journey teases the audience by breaking the fourth wall, foreshadowing an unforgettable grand finale.

Eventually, Pippin grows comfortable with the love he finds in a simple woman and her son but is convinced by the Leading Player to leave, that there is more to life than his great love. His love interest, Catherine, goes off-script because she wants Pippin to stay with her. This angers the Leading Player, since the troupe is supposed to stick to the script. He isolates Pippin, who feels purposeless and overwhelmed in his search for meaning. The Leading Player convinces him that he can fulfill his purpose and leave a lasting impact by taking part in the grand finale, an act where Pippin will jump into a pit of fire and become one with the flame.

Pippin knows the consuming fire will kill him, but the Leading Player and troupe perform a grand number to convince him this is the only way to find some sort of meaning and fulfillment to life. Just before he jumps into the blazing pit, Pippin realizes there has to be more to life than death. It can't be meaningless, right? There must be more than just aimlessly seeking some sort of satisfaction in the world, then ending it all with a bang.

Catherine and her son, Theo, rush onto the stage, "interrupting" the show to convince Pippin to leave with them; he complies and abandons his plans to dive into the flames. His purpose was never in the shiny, glittery things the Leading

Player had presented as meaningful, but in the ordinary life and love he'd found.

The Leading Player becomes enraged by this defiance and begins to tear apart the whole set—the costumes, lights, live orchestra, and everything visible onstage—before retreating. Only Pippin, Catherine, and Theo remain onstage, singing together as a family. Then, as Catherine and Pippin leave, Theo rummages through scraps of the torn-up set left behind. He sings the same song Pippin sang at the show's beginning, about finding his place in the world and meaning in life, when the Leading Player and troupe reenter; and the audience witnesses the destructive, seductive cycle start again.

That is how I interpreted the show, at least, so Bob Fosse and Roger O. Hirson, forgive me if I misinterpreted your wonderful musical production. It's my favorite production because the antagonists are so like Satan and his demons. At the beginning of the show, the singing, dancing, acrobatics, and performances are so mesmerizing. You truly feel as though the Leading Player and troupe are there to help Pippin in his journey of discovery and purpose, only to discover they want to destroy him.

As humans, the biggest questions we wrestle with are our purpose, our sense of meaning, and our place of belonging, all of which God can answer since He is our Creator and Designer. He knows our main function and reason for existence. He is the One who made us on purpose and with a purpose—that's why He knows what is best for us and gives us instruction, guidance, and boundaries so we can live in actual freedom. However, Satan is on a mission to destroy, distance, and distract us from finding our meaning in God and thriving in our relationship with Him. He wants us off-route. He wants us to crash and burn.

The Origins of Our Opposition

With all the assumptions and caricatures in the world about the Enemy, I want to clarify his *actual* identity and where he came from. He goes by many names: Satan, Lucifer, the devil. Call him whatever you want, but know that he is no good, unlike our good God. Let's compare the two.

God is the Creator (Nehemiah 9:6); Alpha and Omega (Revelation 22:13); the eternal, sovereign Author of all life (Colossians 1:16–17); and has always existed (Psalm 90:2). Colossians 1:16 details this about Him: "For everything was created by him, in heaven and on earth, the visible and the invisible, whether thrones or dominions or rulers or authorities—all things have been created through him and for him" (CSB). All things, including the angels and heavenly things, were created by God. Being a fallen angel himself, Lucifer is a created being (Ezekiel 28:13) who had a beginning and will be put to an end (Revelation 20:10), is not sovereign (John 14:30), and offers death rather than life (Hebrews 2:14).

I promise you that angels aren't quite like what you've seen in Renaissance paintings. They aren't little naked babies with plump bellies and harps, feeding grapes to royalty whenever they have time off from worshiping God in His throne room. Angels are ministering spirits (Hebrews 1:14; Psalm 148:2). Their ministry to God involves praising and worshiping Him alone (Isaiah 6:2–3; Psalm 103:20) and carrying out His purposes through blessing, intervening with, and judging humanity. Two key words describe angels in the Bible: the Old Testament Hebrew word *malak*, meaning "sent one" or "messenger," and the New Testament Greek word *angelos*, meaning "angel" or "messenger." So angels are messengers—the good ones and the bad ones.

Bad angels? Kirby, do you mean demons? Yep, I do.

You know what I find interesting? A lot of mainstream music artists sing about demons. I specifically recall my first Imagine Dragons concert where they sang their song "Demons," with the lyrics, *"Don't get too close / It's dark inside / It's where my demons hide."*[1] And *"Look into my eyes / It's where my demons hide."*[2] At first, I just sang along to these lyrics because they were mainstream radio hits. But when I heard the group sing at that concert, I really began to listen and wondered if the lyrics were true for them. Did they feel oppressed by demons? I'm not talking about head-spinning, exorcist-type possession, but feeling exploited and enslaved by the attacks of Satan and his evil messengers.

All I know is that I don't want to befriend or hang out with Satan and his demons, thank you. Perhaps all these artists are plagued by demonically inspired anxiety and depression; suicidal ideations; loneliness; greed; paranoia; and harmfully intrusive, destructive thoughts. It's pretty telling that we see this in the music industry, especially since Satan initially oversaw music and worship as an angel (Ezekiel 28:13). Regardless, I know that despite the attacks, the oppression, and the torment, the simple name of Jesus makes demons shudder and flee. *Jesus, Jesus, Jesus!* There is power and freedom in that name, and Satan knows that too.

Satan's Method

Satan's method is to lie, deceive, accuse, isolate, and destroy.

He exploits our wants, desires, and deepest wishes in an

attempt to convince us that any way contrary to God's way will satisfy our hungry soul. That is his method—to derail us through deception and twisted reasoning that isn't really reasonable at all, because it always leads to the same thing: defeat, humiliation, shame, anger, isolation, emptiness, and self-loathing.

When I think about the times I've sinned, I see a clear pattern. Satan deceives me with empty promises, I give in to those lies, and then I end up feeling horrible about what I've done. Maybe after your last one-night stand, you had a pit of self-loathing in your stomach. Maybe after you got the last word in that argument and drove your insult into someone's heart like a knife, it came back to bite you with humiliation looming over your head. Maybe you secretly envy the person you've been bad-mouthing to your friends, and that has only made your insecurity and emptiness grow. Sin feels good for a second, but the spiraling descent afterward is heavy and horrible.

There are a few encounters in Scripture where Jesus went off on people. The peaceful Lamb of God has a backbone, friend, and I am here for it! In John 8:44, Jesus spoke to a particular group of Jews who were in direct opposition to His teachings and ministry. He said to them, "You are of your father the devil, and your will is to do your father's desires. He was a murderer from the beginning, and does not stand in the truth, because there is no truth in him. When he lies, he speaks out of his own character, for he is a liar and the father of lies" (ESV).

Let's focus on the defining statement Jesus made about Satan. Don't glaze over this! He noted that Satan is a *liar*, that there is *no truth* in him, and that he is the *father of all lies*. I have become far too familiar with that voice myself: the lies of the Enemy. Wouldn't you agree?

YOU CAN BE FREE

Here are some lies the Enemy has spun to me:

- I have no value because of what I've done and what's been done to me.
- I am disqualified from doing mighty things because of my shortcomings.
- These distractions are more enticing than true joy; I should move toward them and deviate from the things of God that give me life.
- If I just take matters into my own hands, I will finally feel a sense of control.

Satan appeals to us through appealing things, but he misses the mark, because no matter how "good" it sounds *to* us, it's not truly good *for* us. Let me say it this way: if the Enemy claims that x, y, and z are good for you and me, yet they go against the promises and instruction of God's good, pleasing, and perfect Word, then it's a no for me. I have learned Satan's native language: lies. Whereas God's character is truth (John 14:6; Hebrews 6:18), the Enemy's nature is deceit (John 8:44; 2 Corinthians 11:3, 14). This makes sense considering how the Greek name for devil, *diablos*, means "slanderer." His words, flattery, and false promises are not to be trusted.

A slanderer makes false allegations about other people and lies about their character. I saw way too much of this foolishness in high school. It was beyond tea and hot gossip—which isn't godly either, I might add—it was people ruining the reputation and character of others. I saw classmates plant seeds of lies, half-truths, and falsified stories in the garden of other people's minds so they would have a change of heart toward someone else. I detest that kind of behavior because it is devilish. To see that behavior hurt friends of mine, and even myself at times, was the worst. If those slanderers had just come to them, or to me, I could have told and shown them the truth about my heart, my intentions, and my character. Sadly, we are quick to believe lies rather than test them to see if they contain any truth.

The devil does this all the time—slandering you, me, and God. Much like Regina George, the devil is a *mean girl*.

How Satan Flips the Script on You

Not only is the Enemy a liar and a deceiver; he is also an accuser. Have you ever seen the cartoon of a horse led by a carrot it can't reach, dangling in front of its nose? The person on the horse is holding the stick with the carrot, steering the horse in the direction they want it to go. I feel like the Enemy does this to us, deceiving us with promises that appeal to our eyes, our flesh, and our desires, only to lead us into a pitfall where we wind up stuck, ten feet deep with no way out. Funny how the Enemy is our biggest cheerleader one moment, and in the next yanks the rug right out from under us, all the while pointing, laughing, mocking, and accusing us.

He encourages you to visit that one website you swore you'd never pull up again, then shames you once you click off the screen.

He applauds you for going out to that party and getting involved with people your parents warned you about, then heaps guilt and condemnation over your head the following morning.

He cheers you on as you write that comment online to unleash the anger you have toward someone's post, then points the finger at you for being an embarrassment and a disgrace.

Whatever the sin, this is how the Enemy works as an accuser. He feeds you what you want, then flips the script on you. That leads to isolation, the Enemy's next-best weapon after accusation. If he can get you alone, make you feel completely abandoned, or get you to push everyone else away, he will be the loudest voice and most abrasive influence in your ear. He's used isolation to lead me to do some horrible things. He's convinced me at times, through lies, how horrible I am, that I am unredeemable and unlovable, and that I don't deserve to live. That led me to self-harm and to battle suicidal thoughts and tendencies. But by the grace, steadfast love, pursuing presence, and absolute truth of God, I never got to the point of succeeding in my attempts. Jesus saved me, and that is a huge part of my testimony.

If that is you today—if the Enemy is using isolation to get you to agree with his lies and see death as the only escape—the truth is, the only thing needing to die is your fleshly nature. The only thing that should be put in a grave are those old desires, that old way of life you're sick and tired of living out. The Bible puts it this way: "Then he said to the crowd, 'If any of you wants to be my follower, you must give up your own way, take up your cross daily, and follow me'" (Luke 9:23 NLT). Old self? I don't know her. My heathen era? She is six feet under, right where she belongs. That is the only self that should be put to death, because in Christ, we are transformed, called to live as new creations in His marvelous, joyous light.

I am so glad I am alive today. When I was in that dreadful place, I couldn't imagine what my life could be. But God gave me a way out. He said, "Give me your burdens, and I will give you rest" (Matthew 11:28). "Give me your old mistakes and sinful desires, and I will put them to rest" (Ephesians 4:22–24). "I have plans for you, a hope and a future for you, and real life for you" (Jeremiah 29:11). "Will you take my hand and trust me?" (Isaiah 41:10).[3]

Friend, I know how you must be feeling if you are stuck at the bottom of that pit—ashamed, broken, and repulsed by what you've done. Tired. Hopeless because of the sinful habits you're enslaved to. Embarrassed and worn out thanks to the accusatory and taunting voice of our enemy. I remember sitting in Spanish class during my undergrad studies after a long night of gratifying myself and sinning without any feeling of remorse. I couldn't focus on the lesson. I was so preoccupied with regret over what I had done the evening before. How far I'd let myself go. I didn't even recognize myself. *Is this who I am now? Is this what I've become? If so, I don't like her. I don't want to be around her.* For the first time in my life, I hated myself on a whole new level. I loathed myself. After a few weeks of wallowing, I finally decided I needed help. I needed to talk to a professional Christian counselor, because I didn't want to be that person anymore. I didn't want to feel that way about myself. I wanted to be the confident, free, life-loving Kirby again. And eventually, over time, I got back to that place.

I confess all this to you because I don't want you to give up. Don't give up on yourself, on your healing, on your future, or on God's power at work in your life. Rather, give up your ways for the ways of Christ. When I saw no way out of my sin, the pain, self-hatred, and hopelessness were so heavy I didn't think I could live with them. Ending myself seemed like the only means of release and escape. But that is not true, friend. That is exactly what the Enemy wants you to believe, since he's on a mission to steal, kill, and destroy you (John 10:10). Instead, Jesus offers us life to the full. So put to death everything that is stealing from you, killing you, and destroying you, and allow Christ to start a fresh work in your life, so you can live it for Him.

How to Push Back Death Threats from the Enemy

Jesus' most famous sermon was the Sermon on the Mount, and He kicked it off by teaching the Beatitudes. Let's glance over them and see how they can help us respond to the Enemy's death threats to our lives. Jesus said to the crowds in Matthew 5:3–4, "Blessed are the poor in spirit, for theirs is the kingdom of heaven. Blessed are those who mourn, for they shall be comforted" (ESV). To be *poor in spirit* is to recognize that apart from God, we are helpless in saving ourselves from our sinful ways. Those who understand that they need to depend on God and be connected to Him are deemed *blessed* by Jesus. Likewise, those who mourn are blessed. I've heard this verse used at many funerals and during times of grief. I heard it plenty of times at the passing of my father and my mother. While of course it's true that God is close to the brokenhearted and comforts those who weep in times of grief, that is not the *only* application of this verse. Jesus is mainly speaking to those of us who mourn our *sins*.

I remember thinking, *How did I get to this place?* when I struggled with my porn addiction. Years and years had passed with me trying my best to stop, only to fail once again—keeping up a winning streak, then suddenly stumbling out of bounds after one weak compromise. It hurt my heart and put a pit of despair in my stomach when I sinned. My soul grieved traveling to that place again. I think it upset me so greatly because after coming to Christ, I finally understood the reality of sin and how it affected me, my pursuit of God, and others. You and I both know how that feels. But friend, Jesus doesn't want to leave us in that pit of pity and groaning. He doesn't want you hiding your face and suffering in silence moments after or the morning after. Once we've recognized our sins, Jesus wants us to repent and call on Him to rescue us from the habits that are killing us.

ONCE WE'VE RECOGNIZED OUR SINS, JESUS WANTS US TO REPENT AND CALL ON HIM TO RESCUE US FROM THE HABITS THAT ARE KILLING US.

God has plans (Jeremiah 29:11), purposes (Romans 8:28), freedom (Galatians 5:13), and fullness (John 10:10) for you. Don't let the Enemy take your life. Don't let him deceive you into believing there is no way out of the trap he tricked you into. Don't let him convince you that *It worked for Kirby, but it won't work for me.* Our enemy understands, probably more than you right now, how much of a force you are to be reckoned with under the authority, power, and provision of God. Compared to our mighty God, Satan is weak, puny, and defeated. Don't let the Enemy take you out. Hear me loud and clear: Satan is a liar, a deceiver, an accuser, an isolator, and a destroyer. Whatever he wants for us is no good, and we should not entertain anything he offers us, whether it's a seemingly sweet dangling carrot or an opportunity to opt out of the abundant life God has prepared for us to live.

Satan's Mistake

Satan makes the mistake of ignoring the fact that Christ has already won.

Won what exactly? He defeated the power of sin and death over our lives (which separated us from Him) by conquering death itself on the cross. Jesus calls Himself the way, the truth, and *the life* in John 14:6. He is fully God by nature and fulfilled the requirements of the Old Testament Law (which God used to judge mankind at the time). Jesus was able to die in our place and resurrect three days later because He is the Alpha and the Omega, the God of all creation. There was no way in hell that hell could defeat Jesus. There was no way on earth the devil could put to death the Author of Life Himself. Jesus not only conquered death with His crucifixion, burial, and resurrection, but He imputed (passed on) that victory to all who believe in Him. We get to share in the benefits of Christ's victory: "But thanks be to God, who gives us the victory through our Lord Jesus Christ" (1 Corinthians 15:57 ESV). We win. You win. You get to live a life of freedom because Jesus won!

WE WIN. YOU WIN. YOU GET TO LIVE A LIFE OF FREEDOM BECAUSE JESUS WON!

Satan does not want people to know that truth. He tries to convince people that God isn't real, is evil, or doesn't truly love them due to their sins. He knows the truth and wants to hide it from us—because once a person is fully convicted of the real war and the victory available in Christ, they can fight to win. Fighting for victory and fighting from victory look very different.

As believers, we fight the schemes of Satan *from* a place of victory. Death is defeated, the battle is won, and all the Enemy can do now is try his best to distract and deceive us from the truth that sets us free (John 8:32). Because of Christ, we are no longer bound by the Enemy to live in condemnation. Hell is not our home; heaven is.

Seeing Through the Snake

There is nothing good about the Enemy. He is a snake, and not just because he is the serpent in the book of Genesis. He deceives, divides, distorts, and destroys everything and anything he can get his greedy little claws on. If we believe he is evil and his schemes aren't good for us, we need to drill into our minds that the choices he presents shouldn't be reasoned with or rationalized. The second you hear his voice, shut that thing down! We know his native language of lies stands in direct opposition to the truth of God. This is why Scripture is so vital for Christians—it's God's truth, His self-revelation, and our guide to living abundantly with our beloved Creator. Reading the Bible is not a to-do task that makes God love you more; it serves up transformational truths that bring us closer to Christ, empowers us daily, and gives us eyes to distinguish the things of God from those of the Enemy. Being daily refreshed with the truth helps us identify the lies we believe and the desires that deceive us.

Knowing Satan is wicked, a destroyer, and a disrupter of all things good and true, clearly the One he opposes stands for the opposite: all that is true, noble, right, pure, lovely, admirable, excellent, and praiseworthy (Philippians 4:8). It is God, Yahweh, revealed in the Trinity as the Father, Son, and Holy Spirit, who stands for these things. He is the one and only One; He is I AM (Exodus 3:14). The glory, the praise, the authority, the title *Lord* belongs to Him alone. Ephesians 3:20–21 says, "Now to him who is able to do immeasurably more than all we ask or imagine, according to his power that is at work within us, to him be glory in the church and in Christ Jesus throughout all generations, for ever and ever! Amen."

IF WE SEE AND KNOW GOD CORRECTLY, IT CHANGES EVERYTHING: HOW WE LIVE, LOVE, SERVE, AND OVERCOME.

I hope in the next chapter we can see through the snake—the Enemy—and the lies he feeds us, specifically the lies about God. If we see and know God correctly, it changes everything: how we live, love, serve, and overcome. Let's break down those lies about God and lay a new foundation of truth.

BATTLE PLAN STEP #3:
Know Your Enemy

As we move into the next chapter and dive deep into the truth about God, His character, and how we often see Him, I want us to remember the truth about our enemy, who is out to get us:

- Satan is not like our good God. Our enemy has a beginning and an end; is the father of lies; is a deceiver and a destroyer; and attempts to steal, kill, and destroy God's beloved: you and me.

- Satan overpromises and underdelivers by tempting us, then trapping us. He entices us with sin on a silver platter only to lead us into a pit of despair, shame, brokenness, loneliness, hurt, and grief. He has never been on your side, and he certainly doesn't have your best interest in mind.

- Satan cannot destroy those who are in Christ, so instead, he will do everything he can to distract, deceive, and distance you from God, His truth, and the fullness of joy, peace, and life with Christ.

- Although Satan can seem scary and powerful, he fails compared to the power and promises found in Christ and the gospel! Satan is defeated. He doesn't stand a chance against the God we serve, know, and love. He cannot overcome the victories of Christ. The truth is, Christ has won our salvation, our freedom, and our future. Jesus saves, redeems, empowers, and separates us from the entrapment of our former ways. We now see the Enemy for who he is—a fallen angel—and we have the authority of Christ in us to dismiss his lies and temptations.

- Satan and his demons must flee at the name of Jesus. We no longer have to live oppressed or depressed. We can live freed and forgiven in Christ!

CHAPTER FIVE

THE LIES WE BELIEVE ABOUT GOD

Now that we have exposed the Enemy and his motives, mission, method, and mistakes, I want to shift gears and recognize some truths about God. I'm convinced we have a tainted view of God because of our sin and because of the Enemy; sadly, this has been humanity's default since the fall. Genesis 3:7–8 details Adam and Eve's response to their sin: not to walk and talk in the garden with God about what had just happened but to cover up with fig leaves and hide themselves. The fear they felt, the shame they carried, and the lies they believed caused them to keep far away from God instead of running to Him. Can you relate to them? I certainly do.

Whether from lust, lying, anger, or pride, I've also hidden my face from God in shame and fear. It was hard for me to believe that God still loved me, wanted me, and would ever forgive me for my sin. It was easier to run away than face what I had done and admit it to God. I wanted to literally cover myself up so nobody could see what greatly embarrassed me. But here is the awful reality: the darkness allowed my mess to turn into a more harmful and toxic mold. That is exactly where the Enemy wants you—tripped up and hiding your face from the only One who can heal you, speak life and purpose over you, and place new desires within you.

Maybe you have a hard time coming to God because of how your parents treated you when you messed up, or how your pastor shamed you in front of the congregation, or how a Christian friend gossiped and abandoned you. But hear me out—*they are not God.* In fact, I know that their actions toward you broke God's heart. He wants to meet you with empathy, kindness, and gentleness. That's who our God is. The people who hurt us are broken and sinful, just like you and me, and they also need the grace and forgiveness of Jesus for their sins. God is compassionate, faithful, and loving. Not only will He heal that trauma through a gentle and timely process with you, but He will redeem how you see Him as you turn to Him in trust rather than run away and hide.

I view God in a completely different way than I once did, and I am so thankful I know the real Him, the *true* Him. Not what Satan's lies or poor role models made Him out to be. I came to know the one true God, and it changed everything. That's what He wants, friend. For us to really know and be known by Him. In the light He can take that toxic mold and instead mold you into the person He's called you to be: freed and empowered for the plans, purposes, and places He has destined for you.

The Enemy causes us to view God incorrectly.

Sin causes us to view God inaccurately.

Trauma causes us to view God imperfectly.

IT IS TIME TO COME OUT OF HIDING AND INTO HIS SAFEKEEPING.

Mix those things together and we see a God who isn't. I want us to see the God who *is*; the great I AM. Let's begin by recognizing five prominent lies we believe about God that plague believers and nonbelievers, keeping them in bondage and brokenness. We need to reveal the truth of His character and heart to know redemption in our lives. It is time to come out of hiding and into His safekeeping.

Lie #1: God Will Abandon You

Maybe this is where you are stuck today, believing God will abandon you because you made a bad decision, gave in to that temptation, or crossed a boundary you never thought you would cross. I have personally believed this lie—that God no longer wanted to be with me. It is a really discouraging place to be because it not only causes us to feel rejected and forgotten, but those perpetual feelings of loneliness and rejection cause us to seek affirmation and approval from other people, places, and things. They dare to compete with but fail to compare to the assurance and truth found in God.

I never experienced anxiety attacks until I got to college. At first, I didn't know why they were happening. Was it my classes? The new environment? Being independent for the first time? It took months before I realized the cause: I felt like God had abandoned me. I would cry and cry, pray and pray, and demand that God tell me why He felt so far away. I was going to my Bible classes and church, reading Scripture, and doing all the "Christian things" that should have given me peace that God was near. I couldn't eat, and whatever I could eat wouldn't stay down. I ended up weighing less than one hundred pounds by the end of that semester. I felt burdened. Through my own blindness and stubbornness, I was in a relationship with a guy who was not a godly man. Even before we started dating, I felt God say so clearly to me, *Do not date him, Kirby.* My response to that was, "Don't worry, God! I'll be okay!" I felt strongly in my heart that God did not approve of our relationship, but I brushed it off and continued living the way I wanted to. My disobedience and ignoring the conviction He gave me resulted in feeling far from God and assuming He had abandoned me.

Let me just say that when God says no to things, He has very good reasons for doing so. As it turned out, that guy was living a double life I knew nothing about, one not honoring to the Lord at all. For months, he had deceived me. When I found out, I felt so betrayed and broken. The night he and I broke up, I remember praying to God and asking for forgiveness because for months I had ignored His voice. I took His commands as mere suggestions, disrespecting His authority over my life. That explained my feelings; I was dwelling in sin rather than in submission to God. He hadn't abandoned me; *I* had abandoned *Him*. When I finally came to that realization and repented, God didn't scold me. He didn't condemn or ridicule me for messing up and sinning against Him. No, He comforted my broken heart, filled me with peace, and reassured me of the plans He had for me; they have always been far better than my own.

God did not abandon me in my shame, and He didn't leave

Adam and Eve in their shame either. It says in Genesis 3:21, "And the LORD God made clothing from animal skins for Adam and his wife" (NLT). He sacrificed an animal to cover Adam and Eve in their sin. God comes looking for us in our shame and makes a way to cover and cleanse us from our sin through Jesus. He is the ultimate sacrifice for our sin, the final and full covering for our shame. Jesus came to take away your sin, shame, and any separation you feel from God. Hebrews 9:12 says, "He entered once for all into the holy places, not by means of the blood of goats and calves but by means of his own blood, thus securing an eternal redemption" (ESV). Romans 4:7 says, "Blessed are those whose lawless deeds are forgiven, and whose sins are covered" (ESV).

God has not abandoned or deserted you today. He gave you His word that He wouldn't. "The LORD will not abandon his people; he will not desert those who belong to him" (Psalm 94:14 GNT). No matter what you've done, no matter what sin cycle you're stuck in, He is still as near as your next breath and is passionate about a relationship with you. A covenant isn't a contract, friend. A contract has everything to do with behavior, whereas a covenant has everything to do with belief. A contract has everything to do with performance, whereas a covenant has everything to do with a promise.

God so beautifully foretold our covenantal relationship with Him in Ezekiel 36:22–32 as well as in Jeremiah 31:31–34. Those verses detail the hope and promise the entire Bible leads us to: a Savior, Jesus, and the freedom He brings to those once held captive to sin's dominion in life. Sin no longer separates from God those who have professed faith in and devotion to Jesus. Our faith enters us into that covenantal relationship with Christ and gives us confidence and assurance that God will never leave nor forsake us (Deuteronomy 31:8).

Don't believe the lie that God has moved on from you, because He has gone to every extent to have an ongoing, present, covenantal relationship with you from now until eternity. He does not reject you; He wants you. He has never stopped and will never stop pursuing you. Like the good shepherd who left the ninety-nine sheep to go after the lost one, He is on a mission to find and rescue you (Matthew 18:10–14). Return to Him, let go of what's keeping you from Him, and be comforted knowing that He will welcome you with kindness and mercy, not wrath and judgment.

> **HE DOES NOT REJECT YOU; HE WANTS YOU. HE HAS NEVER STOPPED AND WILL NEVER STOP PURSUING YOU.**

The lie: God will leave you behind when you fall into temptation and sin. The truth: God will never abandon you when you make a mistake. He will pursue you, meet you where you are, and cleanse you from your sin and shame, clothing you in His grace. He will draw near even if you have hidden yourself away.

Lie #2: God Is Angry with You and Disappointed in You

I don't know what is worse: having somebody angry with you or disappointed in you. On one hand, you have someone's outrage, displeasure, and resentment headed your way. On the other is a tsunami of guilt, humiliation, and the weight of letting someone's expectations down. Either way, it sucks, and I think we sometimes believe that this is how God feels toward us when we stumble into sin. It reminds me of that unforgettable scene from season 4 of *America's Next Top Model* when Tyra Banks yelled at one of the models she sent home. Whether you watched the show or have seen it as a meme, those famous words were, "I was rooting for you! We were all rooting for you! How dare you! Learn something from this!"[1] The anger Tyra exuded toward this girl stands out to me as a perfect example of disappointment in action. It was awful to watch. It's even worse to feel.

Maybe that is how you believe God sees you. Perhaps that is even the negative self-talk you beat yourself up with when you end up back at square one, trying to overcome that addiction, that temptation, that sin. Maybe you think God sounds a little like this:

Really, again?

Get it together already!

When will you learn?

I really thought you were going to keep your word this time.

You just won't stop, will you?

I'm so fed up with you always messing up.

Those words, those thoughts, those feelings? Yeah, those are things I have desperately struggled with. For the longest time I believed the lie that when God looked at me, He didn't see His beloved, His child, His redeemed. I thought all He saw was a disappointment, unworthy of the call He had placed on my life, undeserving of being in His presence. Knowing my thoughts and mistakes, my broken promises, and where I fell short, I could only imagine how angry He should have been at me.

Sure, maybe His grace was available the first, second, maybe even third time I missed the mark, but after ten times? Twenty?

Two hundred? Two thousand!? How could someone not end up angry and disappointed in me after I swore I would never do it again. If it were an episode of *Dance Moms* and God was like the ruthless dance coach, Abby Lee Miller, I would be kicked off the dance team at that point, stuck at the bottom of the pyramid ranking for that week, or put on probation, trying to work my way back into the spotlight.

Here's the thing, though: I believed this lie because I put an unrealistic expectation on myself to be perfect and never mess up. If I gave my word, I wanted to be faithful to it, but we all know how human we are when it comes to promising we won't ever make a mistake. I had projected that expectation of myself onto *God*, as *His* expectation for me. Rather than viewing myself as God sees and knows me, I put extreme pressure on myself to perform, as if my life and His love for me depended on it.

That mindset sucked the joy out of my relationship with God, making it more about appeasing Him than being pleasing to Him. There is a big difference between the two. One comes from a place of *doing*, the other from a place of *being*. When we truly abide or rest in our relationship with God, our lives become transformed. We are loved as a result of who we are, not what we do. Matthew 3:17 provides a perfect example of this when God said of Jesus, "This is my beloved Son, with whom I am well-pleased" (Matthew 3:17 csb).

We can pull three truths from this verse alone that display the heart of God beautifully and accurately:

1. God declared Jesus beloved.
2. God declared Jesus pleasing to Him.

3. God was pleased with Jesus' perfect faithfulness, yet simply loved Jesus as His Son.

God *loved* His beloved Son even before Jesus' miracles and ministry, friend. If that is how the Father truly views the Son, why wouldn't it be true for those of us now adopted as His sons and daughters? Contrary to how the world around us revolves and operates, what we do doesn't determine who we are; our identity is meant to determine what we do.

Your negative thoughts and the Enemy's toxic lies push you to seek affirmation and a sense of validation, but God already loves you! This is good news! You don't have to *do* anything to earn His love; you simply have to exist. How liberating is that? But don't get it twisted—I am not saying we can just keep on sinning because God loves us regardless. We want to stop sinning because of how God's love moves us!

WHAT WE DO DOESN'T DETERMINE WHO WE ARE; OUR IDENTITY IS MEANT TO DETERMINE WHAT WE DO.

One of the most iconic scenes in *The Lion King* is when Mufasa's voice speaks from beyond the grave and encourages his son, Simba, in saying, "Remember who you are." Simba did not feel worthy. He felt like a disappointment. But his actions didn't define him. He was a king, and the son of a king! That was Simba's identity! I think many of us need to remember who we are and whose we are; we need to cling to what God says about us over the lies that lead us astray. Simply put, to project my negative view of self onto God's perception of me is unfair. It is inaccurate, because that's the opposite of what God says about me and how

He created me. Anything contrary to His words and His work is simply a lie.

Unlike the models on *America's Next Top Model* or the dancers from Abby Lee's dance studio, we, as children of God, are not in a competition. We are not fighting to keep the spot we secured based on last week's performance. Our salvation, in case you forgot, is not something we secured or earned on our own. Salvation and righteousness were imputed to us, given as a free gift by Jesus Himself (Romans 5:6–9). On top of that, nothing can separate us from our new identity as sons and daughters of the Most High King. Romans 8:38–39 assures us of this, saying, "For I am persuaded that neither death nor life, nor angels nor rulers, nor things present nor things to come, nor powers, nor height nor depth, nor any other created thing will be able to separate us from the love of God that is in Christ Jesus our Lord" (CSB).

GOD UNDERSTANDS YOUR STRUGGLES AND WEAKNESSES. HE DOESN'T PUT UNREALISTIC EXPECTATIONS ON YOU.

My friend, please know that God won't give you some long-winded "I told you so" speech and shame you for your cycles of sin. No, He always comes running to meet you with open arms, forgiving you fully, calling you deeper into relationship with Him, because it's there we will grow new desires and fresh love for Him. Carrying shame doesn't lead us away from sin; it keeps us stuck in it. It's His love and truth that spur us on to greater freedom. It's in the deep place with God that He shows you the beautiful plans He has for you, sets you on the right coordinates, and gives you every tool you need to live the life He won for you.

The lie: God is angry and disappointed in you for your

mistakes and mess-ups, only hurling wrath, condemnation, and shame your way. The truth: God understands your struggles and weaknesses. He doesn't put unrealistic expectations on you. He provides you with security and stability, assuring you of your identity in Him when you feel as though you least deserve it. That is the free gift of our salvation and justification—to forever belong to a good, gracious, understanding, and forgiving God.

Lie #3: God Doesn't Love You (Anymore)

I promise I'm not a dinosaur, but it kind of feels that way considering I've been creating content since I was thirteen. I've witnessed fads, trends, the rise of "influencer culture," and the beginnings of "cancel culture." When I first began my social media journey, cancel culture wasn't a thing, at least not what it has evolved into today. Sure, I think a healthy level of accountability needs to be out there with the messages we send and how we behave, but I think it has reached such an extreme that if you blink, you're canceled. If you don't blink, you're canceled. If you say the sky is blue, you're canceled. If you don't think the sky is blue, you're canceled. I have noticed such a deep level of anxiety bred in our culture because of this. People live in fear that whether they say something or don't, their reputation will be tarnished, their follower count will plummet, and the love they once received from so many strangers online will be lost in an instant.

I grew up as a serious people pleaser, so I know social media can be a very dangerous space for seeking love and validation. Why? Because as easy as it is to gain it, it's just as easy to lose.

A person's whole world can crumble because of the acceptance they crave from their followers online. I've seen people thrive off the praise, conform to culture to keep everyone happy, and ultimately lose themselves as they sell out just to stay relevant, loved, and deemed acceptable by the jury of people behind the screens.

Hear me out for a second. I don't want to demonize social media, especially since that is a huge part of my ministry and I love to create on it. I wholeheartedly believe media is the biggest mission field out there, and I have made some of the best friendships and connections through it, including my husband! I love to create, connect, disciple, and reach people online, not to mention share memes that make me laugh until my stomach hurts. However, as someone who has faced backlash, cancel culture, and the disapproval of random strangers online, I understand how toxic it can be if you choose to find your worth there.

People's opinions sway from the left to the right; this is something Jesus knew personally. Those worshiping Him on Palm Sunday, shouting, "Hosanna!" as He entered the Jerusalem gates (John 12:13), were the same ones yelling, "Crucify Him!" just a few days later (Luke 23:21). He knows how fickle man's feelings and opinions are, and He understands the conditional love extended and taken away in our world. But that is not how He chooses to love us, nor was that His original design for how we are to love one another.

I think we view God's love for us through that worldly lens because of society's example of conditional love. *If I do this, He will love me. If I don't do this, He won't love me anymore.* It's like a schoolgirl plucking the petals off a flower at recess. It is no wonder that when we disobey God and go against His instruction and plans, we get sucked into the lie that He must no longer love us. That's what we are so used to seeing. But God models unconditional love. Perhaps you've heard these verses before, but I really want you to take a minute to hear what it says:

> "For God so loved the world, that he gave his only Son, that whoever believes in him should not perish but have eternal life. For God did not send his Son into the world to condemn the world, but in order that the world might be saved through him." (John 3:16–17 ESV)

My friend, Jesus did not come to heap condemnation on you. The fact of the matter is, apart from Jesus, *we* condemn *ourselves*. Each of us, being human like Adam and Eve, was born with a sinful nature. Parents out there, you know you don't have to teach a toddler to misbehave. Because of our sinful actions, we all stand guilty before a perfect God. However, because God loved us so greatly, He sent His Son, Jesus, to pay off the debt of our sin, to negate our sinful nature and cover the cost of everything we broke. Any offense we previously had is washed away by the blood of Jesus when we receive His salvation. He came to save us from the sin that entangles us and the separation that comes from our disobedience. Jesus doesn't want you to be condemned, so He did something about it. He fixed the problem! He became the bridge to bring us back to God! He is the singular doorway we enter through to escape that pit of condemnation, self-hatred, and judgment and begin a relationship with God defined by love, forgiveness, and freedom.

I remember weeping in front of my most recent counselor because I felt condemnation over a specific sin that was crushing me. I had made a foolish mistake. I knew better. And because of that, I believed the lie that God no longer loved me or wanted to be close to me. I *truly* believed I was unlovable and unredeemable. Perhaps that's what you are convinced of today for yourself. My counselor reminded me that as Christians, we no longer operate under condemnation. Imagine two buckets: one labeled "Condemned" and the other labeled "Saved." When you profess Jesus as your Lord and Savior, receive forgiveness for your sins through His death on the cross, and submit to His will for your life, God removes you from the Condemned bucket and places you in the Saved one. Those who have been justified by the cross cannot be removed from the new bucket, column, category, place, or whatever you want to call it. We *remain* saved even if we struggle with sin. As we continue to remain in Him, pursue Him, and steadfastly endure despite the obstacles of sin and temptation, God is faithful to keep us. First Corinthians 1:8–9 promises us this: "He will also keep you firm to the end, so that you will be blameless on the day of our Lord Jesus Christ. God is faithful, who has called you into fellowship with his Son, Jesus Christ our Lord."

So why do we continue to live and act as if we are still condemned? We aren't, so we shouldn't! It's silly for us to live in fear, dread, and hopelessness because the work of the cross is final and permanently marks our lives. We get to live in freedom and forgiveness because of Christ.

I want to make a clear distinction here, though. Just because we are no longer condemned by our sin (that is, sentenced to a life separated from God eternally) does not mean we don't experience *conviction*. Maybe you are confusing that feeling of conviction with condemnation. Condemnation involves *sentencing*, whereas conviction comes as a *sensing*. The Greek word for *conviction* is *elencho*. It means "to convince someone of the truth; to reprove; to accuse, refute, or cross-examine a witness."[2] It is not just an awareness of right versus wrong like with our conscience. The Holy Spirit reveals to us the truth of our sin before a Holy God. When we understand what is pure versus what is wicked, we naturally respond to our sin with loathing. As John 16:8 explains, the Holy Spirit brings about conviction within the world. He brings us to a place of mindfulness and realization we cannot shake off. He will faithfully convict us of any behavior, thinking, or choice that is not glorifying to God, good for us, or in alignment with what is right.

When you sin as a Christian, you naturally feel conviction, not condemnation. If you experience conviction for your sin, congratulations! That's good! The Holy Spirit is within you, revealing truth to you and giving you a clear view of what you need to repent from to restore a vibrant walk with God. Out of His love and mercy He convicts us of sin, course correcting us to a life of freedom and fullness.

The lie: God does not love me, and even if He once did, He no longer does because of the mess and mistakes I've made in my life. I must work to earn His love and approval and live in fear of condemnation and rejection. The truth: God loves me. He showed His greatest display of that unconditional love on the cross through Jesus' sacrifice. In His love, He has given me the Holy Spirit as a guide to convict and correct me so I can enjoy the fullness of life He has for me and the love He wants to continue to show me. He so loves me and so loved the world that He withheld nothing to save and sustain us. His love covered my sins and still does.

Lie # 4: He Expects You to Be Perfect

Tell me if you can relate to any of these thoughts or beliefs:

Since I am saved, God now expects perfection from me.

Since I have made Jesus my Lord and Savior and understand the weight and ramifications of sin, I will no longer sin . . . right?

If I fall short of that expectation, God will see me as a failure.

Is that the narrative in your head, plaguing you with performance anxiety and taking the joy out of an authentic relationship with Christ? Even after being saved for over a decade, there were seasons in my walk with Christ when I believed this lie about God's heart, character, and nature. I don't know when that seed was planted in my mind, but I sure watered it until it bore bad fruit that affected my relationship with God. The idea of living sin-free gave me the worst anxiety and made me feel hopeless. I simply couldn't do it. My attempts at micromanaging my mistakes began to steal the spotlight from Jesus and made me the savior of my life. I relied on my self-sufficiency to sustain me, leading to a lifestyle that kept me from leaning on Him. Whenever I suddenly sinned, I felt like I had completely failed God, and I was too ashamed to face Him because of it. I thought I had to clean up my mess before I came to Him, or just flat-out not have any mess at all. The pressure to perform and be perfect was crippling.

My longest porn-free streak, aside from where I am today, lasted eleven months. I almost made it a whole year. I was so proud of myself for not acting upon my impulses, shutting down my devices at a good time, and making sure I stayed busy whenever I had those urges. What I failed to do, though, was *rely on the Lord*. Those eleven months were all about relying on my own strength. My efforts seemed pretty impressive, but not compared to today. I have been porn-free since 2016, thanks to the strength Jesus gives me to resist temptation and fight the Enemy's lies with the truth and tactics I'm sharing in this book.

I thought I had done a good job of cleaning up my act and becoming pristine before the Lord. However, I was exuding all my own energy and strength to sustain myself, and in one night of weak willpower, I caved, beginning a weeklong binge of giving in to my lustful thoughts and desires. I was mortified and didn't want God to be disgusted with me. I didn't want to disappoint Him. I thought, *Next time, I just need to try harder and do better.*

This began a vicious cycle of performing for God, trying to return to my "pre-spiral" state with Him. Although I authentically attempted to "be good" and "do what a Christian should," it made me a slave to my efforts. A slave to the Law. Maybe you've come across this concept while reading the New Testament: in Christ, we are no longer under the constraints of the Law or *slaves* to it. The entire book of Galatians, written by the apostle Paul to the church of Galatia, addresses the issue of Jewish Christians being justified by the finished work of Christ, not their continuous works under the Law—something they seemed enslaved to. Those believers were once subject to the Law, striving to uphold its commands to be made right before God. However, the true purpose of the Law was not to justify people but to reveal to them just how much they needed a Savior, as we do today.

Galatians 3:23 says, "But before the time for faith came, the Law kept us all locked up as prisoners until this coming faith should be revealed" (GNT). The "coming faith" that has been revealed is our faith in Christ! His death, burial, and resurrection have redeemed our sins entirely. You and I no longer have to try to perform to get right with God. Jesus makes us righteous before God! Because of that, we commit our lives to Him, choose to obey Him daily, and meet His grace whenever we fall short.

IT'S NOT ABOUT BUILDING UP LONG STRETCHES OF PERFECT BEHAVIOR; IT'S ABOUT BUILDING UP DAILY STRENGTH FROM REAL RELATIONSHIP WITH CHRIST.

It's not about building up long stretches of perfect behavior; it's about building up daily strength from real relationship with Christ. That leads to sustainable holiness. His perfection makes us holy (set apart from sin), and our daily relationship with Him helps us to keep choosing Him over any temptation the devil throws our way.

One of my former professors at DBU, Dr. Amber Dyer, made this profound statement in class one day: "We are all *falling* in a *rising* elevator." Her husband coined this phrase, saying that it perfectly describes what daily life with Jesus looks like and what sanctification often feels like from a fallen human's perspective. *Sanctification* is one of those fancy Christian words you might hear in a Sunday sermon, but it's a word you and I both need to know in order to grow. Sanctification is the process of Christ perfecting us daily to look more like Him and the person He created us to be. Like a sculptor with a block of marble, we allow Christ to chip away all that doesn't need to dwell in our lives any longer, slowly revealing the creation underneath. Sanctification takes time, and it's something we grow in daily— denying our old ways, letting Christ reveal what needs to go and what needs to grow. Like the sculptor, Christ patiently, precisely, and perfectly works in our life to carve and mold us into the people He destined us to be.

That is exactly what the Dyers meant with the elevator analogy. We are growing—or *rising* in this sense—making progress in our walk with Christ in our intimacy, maturity, conviction, and conduct. However, as humans, we still stumble, make mistakes, and *fall* in this rising elevator. It can feel like we've made no progress when we slip up, but the rising elevator would say otherwise. Jesus understood this struggle for us and even told His disciples in Matthew 26:41,

SANCTIFICATION TAKES TIME, AND IT'S SOMETHING WE GROW IN DAILY— DENYING OUR OLD WAYS, LETTING CHRIST REVEAL WHAT NEEDS TO GO AND WHAT NEEDS TO GROW.

"Watch and pray so that you will not fall into temptation. The spirit is willing, but the flesh is weak." Our spirit is willing to do what is good and right in the eyes of the Lord. Our flesh, however, is in constant opposition to our new desires, trying to trip us up alongside the Enemy's attempts.

I think it's comforting to know that Jesus understands this; He gets that we are willing, but weak. But you know what God affirms about our weakness? Like He said to Paul in 2 Corinthians 12:9, "'My grace is sufficient for you, for my power is made perfect in weakness.' Therefore I [Paul] will boast all the more gladly about my weaknesses, so that Christ's power may rest on me." Where we are weak, we can turn to our Savior and boast in His great power, provision, and presence in our lives. God doesn't expect perfection from us. You know why? Because He knows we aren't perfect! Remember, He made you! He knows your silly quirks, what makes you laugh, what gets under your skin, and even what pulls your attention away from Him. He knows we still struggle with temptation and sin, that it's a real battle we face daily. Our response, however, should not be to flee in fear of failure, burdening ourselves to clean up before we see Him. God doesn't expect this; instead, He asks us to depend on and run to Him when we fall short. He'll willingly, joyfully, and readily aid us in our sanctification journey. He wants to partner with you and help shape, sculpt, and mold you into your best self, into the image-bearer He created.

The lie: God expects you to be perfect, to never sin, and to have it all together, especially if you claim to be a Christian. The truth: God understands our fallen state as humans and takes us through a grace-filled process of sanctification. He walks with us to help us clean up our messes, forgives us, and perfects us, empowering us to grow into who He's called us to be. We will not make excuses or allow sin to overtake our lives, but we understand God has enough grace to cover our sin. In those moments of weakness, Christ asks that we simply show up, admit our sin, receive forgiveness, depend on Him, and pursue Him wholeheartedly and obediently again.

Lie #5: He Won't Forgive Me for This Sin

Have you ever heard the cookie analogy at church? The illustration goes like this: Imagine that for every sin you've committed, you receive a cookie. They stack one on top of the next as you commit more sins. From your perspective, glancing at the stack head-on, it probably towers over you, casting a huge shadow filled with regret and guilt. If we were to line up everyone's cookies, many of us would feel better than some and worse than others, but here's the thing: if God were to look down on all of our cookie stacks, what would He see? Not how high our towers are, but one cookie.

You know what this analogy tells us? That even if we have sinned once, in the eyes of God, we are guilty. I think some of us can shrug off certain sins as "not real sins" and others as "life or death sins," but the fact remains that sin is sin, and all sin is held accountable before God. Whether you cheat on a spelling test or cheat on your spouse, lie about why you are running late or lie about relapsing for the seventh time, gossip about the boss everyone hates or slander someone's character online, it's all sin in the eyes of God. I know—*really* encouraging way to kick off this section, Kirby!

I think it's easy for us to look at our stack of cookies and internalize self-hatred, judgment, and unforgiveness toward ourselves for our sin. Maybe it's easy to accept God's forgiveness and grace for the lie you told your coworker about the progress of your project but impossible when it comes to that abortion you had when you were a teenager. Maybe it's easy to let go of the time you disrespected your parents when you were an angsty teenager, but you still punish yourself for breaking up your family due to a past drug problem. We play judge and say, "God, thanks for forgiving me for these things, but *those* things? Unforgivable. You *can't* forgive me for this. You *won't* forgive me for that." But who are we to say what God will or won't forgive? God is the judge of all things since He has set the standard for what is good, righteous, and orderly, and what is unlawful, rebellious, and wicked.

Romans 3:23 says, "For all have sinned and fall short of the glory of God." I believe the Enemy wants us to forget this verse. If he can isolate us from Christian community as well as God, that sense of loneliness will breed shame, silence, and more sin in our life. The Enemy wants to make us feel unforgivable and alone in our struggles, but the truth is, all believers can relate to the struggle for sanctification and the denial of fleshy desires. Every saint has the past of a sinner! Jesus understands the traps the Enemy sets for us. Luke 4:1–13 details the temptation of Christ, and although He never sinned, He did not spare Himself from the human experience, which included understanding this daily struggle. He knows what we go through mentally, physically, emotionally, and spiritually when temptation is presented to us. He also knows the consequences of sin. He knows how we speak to ourselves after we mess up, how we beat ourselves down, how we hold ourselves hostage, how we often punish ourselves.

EVERY SAINT HAS THE PAST OF A SINNER!

Christ never sinned. He lived life perfectly. Yet He took on our punishment for sin through His death on the cross. Mind you, He did not just die for the little white lie you told, or the pack of gum you stole, or the stop sign you rolled through. Christ also died for the gambling addiction you hate, the dishonesty you've had with your business partners, the crime you did the time for, and even the faithlessness you had in God that caused you to run from Him for so many years. Yes, Jesus will forgive that sin coming to mind right now, the one you think separates you from Him. Truth be told, it *once* separated you from Him because sin does separate us from God. However, because Christ laid down His perfect life to die in payment for our sins, when we accept His payment by faith and commit our lives in surrender to Him, we no longer have a severed relationship with God. He reconciles us to God by removing all the sin that once got in the way. We can approach His throne of mercy and be forgiven for all our sin. *All* of it.

I know some people misunderstand Jesus, believing He simply accepts all the sin along with the sinner. He does accept sinners as they are; He invites us to His table, but His heart, hope, and mission is to transform us and free us from sin. The call-and-response Jesus gave to the woman caught in adultery is the same for those of us stuck in sin today: "*Go and sin no more*" (John 8:11 NLT, emphasis added). Jesus does not want us to live in sin or tolerate it. He laid down His life to free us from our sin. He didn't die to stop you from having a fun time; He died to put to death what is killing you.

> **HE DIDN'T DIE TO STOP YOU FROM HAVING A FUN TIME; HE DIED TO PUT TO DEATH WHAT IS KILLING YOU.**

But please note that Jesus didn't speak to the woman with an accusatory tone. He was gentle. "Then Jesus stood up again and said to the woman, 'Where are your accusers? Didn't even one of them condemn you?' 'No, Lord,' she said. And Jesus said, 'Neither do I. Go and sin no more'" (John 8:10–11 NLT). He met her humiliation with compassion. Conviction, yes, but not condemnation. He does the same with us. Kindly, yet truthfully. Lovingly and understandingly. He calls us to live a life changed for the better, because if you know Jesus, you know He is so much better.

Hebrews 8:12 says, "For I will be merciful toward their iniquities, and I will remember their sins no more" (ESV). Psalm 32:5 also says, "I acknowledged my sin to you, and I did not cover my iniquity; I said, 'I will confess my transgressions to the LORD,' and you forgave the iniquity of my sin" (ESV). That is music to my ears. You know why? Because I have been in iniquity and transgression

before. *Iniquity* is a word translated as *sin* but with its own definition. Likewise, *transgression* is also translated as *sin*, yet it has
a definition of its own.

Sin means "to miss the mark"[3] and is summed up in Romans
3:23—falling short of the glory of God. When we disobey God,
go against His commands, and rebel against His design, we sin.
To *transgress* means to willfully trespass or willfully sin. When
someone trespasses on a property, they are crossing a boundary
into territory where they do not belong or have a right to visit.
When we intentionally sin, such as driving fifteen miles over the
speed limit, calling in sick at work to go to the movies, or even
literally trespassing on someone's property when we know the
rules and regulations, that is transgressional sin.[4]

Iniquity, the most bitter of them all, means to deliberately and
premeditatedly sin without regard for repentance.[5] If unrepentant
sin is apparent in a person's life, it can lead to a cycle of more unrepentant sin, developing a habit or lifestyle of rebellion against God.
I am sad to say that I can relate, but I'm at ease to report that God
forgives us of even our iniquity when we finally come to that place
of repentance. King David—you know, the one who was known
as a man after God's own heart—was deep in iniquity when he
slept with Bathsheba, then proceeded to have her husband, Uriah,
murdered to cover up his sin (2 Samuel 11:1–12:15). We aren't the
only people with messy stories; the "greats" of the Bible were just
like the rest of us scoundrels.

But here's the thing. God forgave David of his iniquity when
he confessed and repented. God *promises* to forgive us when we
confess and repent, something we will look into in the next few
chapters. He is merciful, gracious, and forgiving to those who are

willing to acknowledge their sin and surrender it to Him. He can and will wash away any sin and any stain.

We cannot *quantify* God's forgiveness, limiting the number of times He is willing or able to forgive. Similarly, we cannot *qualify* God's forgiveness, deciding which of our sins are forgivable by God and which are not. God is the one who forgives and deems us worthy of forgiveness, even if we do not feel worthy. Trust me, I want to receive God's forgiveness, but sometimes, when I've been deeply involved in sin, it just doesn't seem like forgiveness is something I deserve. God doesn't forgive me because I deserve it, though. He forgives because Jesus

THE CROSS MADE THE ONCE UNFORGIVABLE, FORGIVABLE.

already paid the debt I owed for it, so I can choose to receive full forgiveness when I repent and follow Christ instead of my own desires. The cross made the once unforgivable, *forgivable*.

His mercy doesn't run out like a timer releasing bits of sand. It will not time out! Do not let the accuser discourage you and make you think that God's grace has run out for your sin. Whether you've been struggling for five days, five months, or five years, He still has mercy for you. God will cover you with forgiveness but call you out of that sin, into His presence, to walk in the newness of life He won for you.

The lie: God cannot and will not forgive me for the sin that binds me. I have sinned in this area way too many times, and His grace and goodness have simply run out. The truth: God's mercy covers every single sin, transgression, and iniquity I've gotten caught up in. God promises in His Word that He will forgive me when I confess and repent. He does not meet me with shameful accusations, but rather compassion and grace every time I stumble, lifting me up and helping me walk in the abundant life He provides.

To Know and to Love

More than anything, God wants us to know Him and His nature. As much as He is mighty, sovereign, transcendent, and Lord of all, He is also eminent, gentle, close, and loving toward His beloved: *you*. He wants you to genuinely, intentionally know Him. In Exodus 6:7, God said to Israel, His chosen people, "I will claim you as my own people, and I will be your God. Then you will know that I am the LORD your God who has freed you from your oppression in Egypt" (NLT). Here is your Hebrew lesson for the day: the word *yada*. *Yada* means "knowing or to know," and it is used 873 times throughout the Bible. But this is not simply an intellectual knowing, like two plus two equals four or the current weather outside. *Yada* is a deep and close understanding on a personal, intimate level.

My followers online know me, as the reader of this book you know me, and I have many friends who know me—but my husband *knows* me. He knows things about me nobody else knows, and not just things that I've told him; he has observed me and spent such quality and sacred time with me, available only to him. He knows me like no one else. He knows how to bring me back to earth when I spiral after a long and stressful day of worrying. He knows how to console me when I grieve or if I'm sick. He knows how to bring me joy in the little things, based off small details he has learned about me. He can spot when I feel uncomfortable, when I'm ready to leave a social event, when I am excited and want to speak up, or when I need him to speak up on my behalf. Richard *knows* me. That is *yada*. And Jesus *knows* me far more than my sweet husband, Richard, ever could!

I write all this and go to such lengths to describe this word because God doesn't just want you to know *about* Him, to flip through a few Bible passages and make up your mind about who He must be. To simply sit in on a Sunday sermon and have Him all figured out. No, He is inviting you to personally know Him—to take His hand, feel His heartbeat, know His ways, and understand His will and purpose for your life. He is waiting on the doorstep of your heart, knocking, hoping that you will allow Him in, so He can begin to heal the hurt, the pain, the shame, the habits, and the addictions you have tried to sweep under the rug for far too long.

God was knocking on my heart a lot in college, and a lot in recent years, as I unpacked loads of shame I'd never dealt with. I was afraid to let Him in, thinking He'd never forgive me for not being an A+ Christian. But He didn't want me to be a poster child for religion. He wanted me to be *His* child. When I let the walls come down, along with the tears, He embraced me and met me with compassion. I never felt worthy of it but needed it so desperately to process my pain and grow from my past.

He's not scared by your mess.

He's not intimidated by your bursts of anger or anxiety.

He's not going to ditch you when you're in a pit of despair or derailment.

He's right there. He's with you. He knows you.

No, like, He *really knows* you.

He understands why you do the things you wish you didn't

and how to help you do what you ought to instead. But you have to know Him and allow yourself to be known by Him, to be loved by Him. First John 4:8 states, "Whoever does not love does not know God, because God is love." When you let Him in to the parts you are most scared of showing, you will be surprised how He will meet you with love every time. As a fellow sinner, I understand how hard it is to let God love you at times, to let Him know what has been happening behind the scenes, after small group, in between class, on the ride home from work. You're not proud of it, that thing that disturbs you and distances you from Him. But God wants to hear it from you. You need to know that God already knows. And despite all that, He still loves you.

In the next chapter, that's what we'll analyze: *you*. We've become familiar with our enemy, we've come to know our Ally, and now it's time to know all about you. Me. Us. Humanity. Why you do what you do, the day-to-day wrestles and obstacles we face as humans, and how we often handle temptation, sin, and what follows.

BATTLE PLAN STEP #4:
Know Your God

If you are going to overcome temptation, the lies you believe, and the sin you're stuck in, you need to understand the truth about our Creator, the Lord over all things. Let's revisit some of that truth before moving on:

- God will not abandon you because you've stumbled and been sucked into sin (or even dove into it). Rather, He continually seeks you out, even in your sin, because He wants to save you from it and its consequences in your life. He has never left you. He will never leave you.
- God is not disappointed in you or angry at your struggle with sin. He understands what it is like to face temptation and how we often reason with the lies and schemes of Satan. Instead of meeting you with wrath, God will meet you with compassion, kindness, understanding, and forgiveness when you repent and turn to Him.
- God still loves you despite what you've done, who you once were, and where you've been. God is love, and everything He does flows from that. He will not withhold His love from you just because you've fallen and sinned. He will gladly continue to meet you with open arms and will love the hell, the sin, the old fleshly desires out of you.
- God does not expect you to be perfect. As Christians, we go through a process called *sanctification*, where Christ perfects us daily to look more like Him. He is patient with us and understands how we wrestle against our desires, because He

is the One who created us. Remove the burden of perfection from your shoulders. Simply pursue knowing Him more and walking in His will.

- God is willing and able to forgive you of every sin, entirely. He doesn't pick and choose which sins to forgive; neither does He want you to punish and shame yourself for "bigger" versus "smaller" sins. He is faithful and just to forgive anyone who repents and receives Him as their Lord.

- God wants us to view Him rightly. If we see Him truthfully, not through the lens of lies the Enemy, the world, and our previous understanding led us to believe, we can walk in freedom. The truth sets us free from every temptation, lie, deception, and wrong desire, exposing what is fake and affirming that which comes from God.

CHAPTER SIX

WHEN YOU TRY YOUR BEST BUT YOU DON'T SUCCEED

I remember sitting in my counselor's office during my time at DBU as an undergrad student. I had been dealing with loads of anxiety and stress, believing that I was not enough and feeling disappointed that my whole life seemed like a mess. Truthfully, I felt like I needed to have it all together all the time, and struggling with sin as a Christian made me feel like a weak hypocrite. With compassion and empathy after listening to my worries and struggles, my counselor looked at me for a moment. He stood and made his way to the whiteboard in his office. Then, he drew something like this:

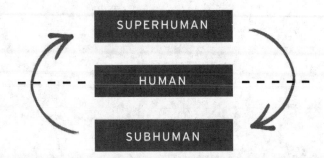

He asked me, "Kirby, do you know what this means?"

I read *superhuman* and *subhuman* on the board, and, confused, replied, "No, I don't."

He explained the vicious cycle that had trapped me in an alternating self-perception of superhuman versus subhuman. A superhuman mentality doesn't involve pride or arrogance, but plays out as a person who holds themselves to a perfect standard, ones who tries to be "enough." What is that standard? How is it measurable? After failed attempts of trying to do it all, be it all, and uphold a perfect image or persona, people collapse hard into the subhuman category: they view themselves as a worthless, insufficient, hopeless disappointment. This sadly fuels the drive to reach for a superhuman level of perfection and performance again to solve the heart's deep longing for acceptance and approval, and to dispel self-hatred and shame. And the cycle continues—climbing and falling, climbing and falling.

Tears streamed down my face, drenching the sleeves of my sweatshirt as I tried to wipe them away. That is *exactly* how I felt about myself. That was *exactly* my pattern. I was trapped: wanting to be enough, to have it all together, to never mess up, so I wouldn't disappoint God. I wanted to be and feel worthy of

His love and the calling on my life. That impossible superhuman expectation only resulted in a deep sense of subhuman failure, as if I were unworthy, unlovable, hopeless, and broken. Before I could even ask my counselor how to escape this, he began to write *human* in the sketch.

He explained, "Kirby, you are not superhuman or subhuman. You are *human*. God made you human. Don't you think that Jesus, God in human flesh, understands what you're feeling and going through right now? You can't put unrealistic expectations of sinlessness and perfection on yourself. You also can't beat yourself up when you are bound to make mistakes. You are a human, and God has enough understanding and grace for you. He knows you. You need to have some of that same grace and understanding for yourself."

Here is the thing, friend: When we become saved, we do not become sinless. A transformation in our hearts and a life of sanctification leads us to *sin less* as we pursue Christ daily. We cannot hold ourselves to an unrealistic expectation of always getting it right. Yes, I certainly believe we should do our best to be above reproach, pursue the things of God, live honorable and holy lives, and deny daily the things that distract and distance us from God. That is what this book is all about! But it is also about the realities of the sanctification process and how God is with us as we separate the old self from the new self. In pursuit of that, we will fail at times. Why? Because we are humans who wrestle with a sinful nature. We have to grow

> WHEN WE BECOME SAVED, WE DO NOT BECOME SINLESS. A TRANSFORMATION IN OUR HEARTS AND A LIFE OF SANCTIFICATION LEADS US TO *SIN LESS* AS WE PURSUE CHRIST DAILY.

to steward our free will in a way that aligns with the will of God rather than our old desires and habits.

A few years after my life-changing counseling session, I heard a sermon by Robert Morris, pastor of Gateway Church, titled "Simply Human."[1] In it, he noted Jesus as the only superhuman. He is perfect! Yet He made Himself human among us so He could fulfill the Old Testament Law, overcome sin, die in our place, and exchange our sin for His righteousness. Because He is superhuman—God, in fact—He rose back to life three days after His crucifixion, defeating sin and death and bringing new life and new hope to those of us enslaved by the things of this world.

Jesus is the superhuman.

> Who, being in very nature God, did not consider equality with God something to be used to his own advantage; rather, he made himself nothing by taking the very nature of a servant, being made in human likeness. And being found in appearance as a man, he humbled himself by becoming obedient to death—even death on a cross! Therefore God exalted him to the highest place and gave him the name that is above every name, that at the name of Jesus every knee should bow, in heaven and on earth and under the earth, and every tongue acknowledge that Jesus Christ is Lord, to the glory of God the Father. (Philippians 2:6–11)

Jesus did what we could not do! He also understands what it is like to be human; He lived it to bring glory to God and the saving gospel. We're all simply human. Have grace for yourself. Have grace for your past self as well—the one who did not understand the depths and realities of your sin. Christ does not expect us to be perfect overnight. He is understanding, compassionate, and kind alongside His correction and guidance. Stop putting unrealistic pressure on yourself and start fixing your eyes and efforts on knowing Christ more, because in doing so, His desires will become yours, His ways will be made known in your life, and the former things will start to fade

PERFECTING, NOT PERFECTION, IS GOD'S METHOD OF MATURING BELIEVERS IN CHRIST ON THEIR FREEDOM JOURNEY.

as He chips away the dead weight. Perfecting, not perfection, is God's method of maturing believers in Christ on their freedom journey. If you're willing to come along for that ride, you have to accept you are simply human—a lesson I'd forgotten I learned at age fourteen.

A Sinner Who Needed Saving

"Don't know what to do with your kids this summer? Send them to Sky Ranch, with all things fun, waterslides, and Jesus!" At least, that's what I think it said. My mother had heard that ad on the radio while trying to figure out what to do with my brother and me for the summer. This happened just after my parents' divorce, when I was eight. Next thing I knew, I was signed up for camp and bunking in Cabin 10. For the first time ever, I had my own Bible and heard the gospel. I wanted to know who this Jesus guy was. The waterslides were pretty awesome, but the feeling of joy and peace covering me in that place was the most enthralling part about it. It wasn't until I was fourteen, though, that I recognized this as the presence of God at that camp, and that I needed Jesus to be my Savior. I needed some saving.

Contrary to the Christian-camp stereotype, I did not give my life to Jesus at the Friday night bonfire boohoo fest. It happened during a Wednesday night worship session right before our evening activity, as I sang all the same songs of summers prior. I simply had a deep longing for more.

For context, during the school year before that particular summer at camp, I had been severely bullied and became extremely depressed and suicidal, and I started to self-harm. Nobody knew, because I was the happy-go-lucky girl, always there to brighten everyone else's day and make sure their burdens weren't crushing them. This left me vulnerable to being the one crushed. I didn't feel like my life had any value or purpose, and my bully doubled down on those lies. I felt empty, unessential, and that my life had no worth. But on those terrible evenings with my note written out, my plan ready to execute, and the readiness to take my last breath, there was always a little voice in the back of my head pleading with me, *One more day. Just give it one more day.* After arguing with the voice, I'd agree, living "one day" at a time for an entire year until that summer before high school. Little did I realize God was speaking to me, saving my life, because He knew I had worth and He had made me for a purpose.

During that Wednesday worship night I realized that I was only truly joyful and free at this camp, learning about Jesus, reading daily devotionals, and attending Bible studies—after the waterslides, of course. I cried out to God and told Him I was only happy there, in His presence, that I was so tired of and exhausted by living life one day at a time instead of truly living with joy, peace, and purpose. I heard God speak to me—not audibly but loudly and clearly in my spirit. I felt it in my bones. It was the most real experience I've ever had, and I can only genuinely describe that moment of my life as *euphoric*. I physically felt God's presence surround me, like I was encased in a warm, bright light. In that awe I heard Him say with such care and concern, *Kirby, what are you doing?* I knew what He meant. Why was I trying to be everything for everyone, pretending to be the happy girl while suffering inside, taking on the impossible responsibility for everyone's well-being, as if I could be their savior. He saw my brokenness, my tiredness, my strain, and my pain. Why was I trying to do what only He could?

He then showed me a sort of slideshow, where He had been present all my life, from the divorce of my parents to the death of my father, and even in my depression. He showed me where He was, how He had protected me, and how He had preserved me from ending my own life. It was as if He looked at my heart, surrounded by brick walls I had built up to protect myself, and gently removed them one by one to get to me. To heal me. To love me. To set me free. Then He spoke this to me, and I will never forget it: *I am your perfect Father in heaven who loves you and is present.* I began to weep. God filled the emptiness I had always felt in my life with His mercy and love. I responded, "I am so tired, God. I want to be freed from this depression. I want to follow You and live for You! What do I do?"

Give it to me, He said. Everything. He wanted it all. My heart, my time, my affection and attention, the burdens I carried, the roles I had tried to fulfill, my struggle with depression, my need to please everyone. He wanted me to release it all to Him. As if removing a rock-filled backpack from my back, I took off everything I had been carrying, and I saw myself laying it down before the cross. Instantly, I was free. My release released me. He released me.

The weight of my depression, my self-harm, my suicidal thoughts and tendencies—it disappeared. I was immediately filled with a newfound spirit of joy, a desire for life, and a conviction to make His name known. I submitted my life to His lordship. I wanted Him to be in charge, because I could not do it. I vowed to live the rest of my days following Him, knowing there would still be hard days, but that I would no longer be alone in my suffering.

I am so glad my camp counselors did not shy away from explaining that to me. Outside of camp, I would be met with the real world, with real struggles and real opposition from the Enemy and others. When that mountaintop feeling faded, God would still be with me in the mundane moments that required faithfulness over feelings. I felt prepared and aware—even though I was justified by my faith in Jesus as my Savior, I still would have to mature and endure. I knew I had sin to overcome and battles I'd have to face. I would need to trust in Jesus as He reshaped me into the person He had called and created me to be. There was work to do. Normal life resumed once I returned home that Saturday afternoon, but I knew God had forever changed me.

Sadly, many Christians don't receive that sobering reminder that once you get saved, there will still be struggles in life and sin to overcome. Yes, we are free from the judgment of our sins, and the Holy Spirit empowers us to resist temptation, but we will still face temptation and have to learn how to navigate our new life. God's timing is truly perfect, because when I got home from camp that summer, a good friend of mine invited me to her youth group. I knew in my heart that I needed to get involved in a church and surround myself with Christian community. Without hesitation, I said yes.

The youth pastor, Jared Lyons, became one of the biggest and best influences in my life, not just as a pastor but as a mentor and father figure I had always hoped to have. To this day, I keep up with him; his incredible wife, Ali; and their beautiful children. He showed me what it looked like to read the Bible and pursue God and what it meant to be a disciple who followed Jesus, put His preaching into practice, and live out the calling and commands He had for my life.

One Wednesday night, Jared preached out of the book of James. I honestly couldn't tell you the points from that message or what the sermon was specifically about, but I began reading James that night, and it quickly became a favorite of mine. The book of James was written by Jesus' brother. Imagine Jesus being your *sibling*. I know we're called brothers and sisters in Christ, but that's through spiritual adoption. James was the *literal* brother of Jesus—that's insane to me. Anyway, the book of James focuses on encouraging believers to not only receive justification by faith but to show the reality of our faith by how we live. Our works do not justify us before God, but they serve as proof and evidence that the Spirit of God is within us and at work in our lives.

While reading James that evening, I came across my life verse. By this, I mean a verse central to who I am and what God has called me to do: "Instead you ought to say, 'If the Lord wills, we shall live and do this or that'" (4:15 NKJV). Whatever God wills and desires for me, my response should be obedience. We obey because we love. We say yes to God's will because we trust His guidance and character. We step where He says to step and let go when He says to let go because we know His ways are

WHATEVER GOD WILLS AND DESIRES FOR ME, MY RESPONSE SHOULD BE OBEDIENCE.

far better than ours. That is the heart behind James 4:15, and I still hold fast to its principles to this day. That's not to say I have always been faithful to it. I have disobeyed plenty. I am a sinful human, just like you—and Adam, Eve, Noah, Abraham, Jacob, David, Peter, and Paul. Just like everybody ever. I have been tempted by my desires and have seen so much regret and disorder result from poor decisions I've made.

It makes me think of an earlier verse in James. "But each one is tempted when he is drawn away by his own desires and enticed. Then, when desire has conceived, it gives birth to sin; and sin, when it is full-grown, brings forth death" (1:14–15 NKJV). Not a very fun verse, I know, but it is true. It's actually a really good picture when you break it down. We conceive sin when we decide to engage in temptation. When we flirt with darkness and choose to hook up with it, we end up giving birth to sin. That sin eventually grows into death, destruction, and disorder in our lives. It affects our relationships with others and with God, and it skews our view of self from who God says we are and who He created us to be. As we allow ourselves to give in to temptation and permit sin to grow in our lives, other things begin to grow within us, too, such as shame, regret, hopelessness, self-hatred, anger, frustration, confusion, and the like. I don't know if you've ever had to fight the urge to stop talking to a toxic ex, but that's what it feels like to cut ties with our old desires and not answer those belligerent DMs the Enemy sends us. It's hard to not pick up the phone to see what he sent us, but if we know the Enemy like we know a toxic ex, then we know it won't end well. It's not worth entertaining.

Jesus Was 100% Human Too

Being human is hard, and quitting our old ways is even harder. The beauty of Christ, however, is that He is *fully God* but also *fully human.* He never sinned, never gave in to temptation, and because of that, He was able to live a perfect life and take our punishment upon Himself, to exchange our sin for His righteousness: "For the sin of this one man, Adam, caused death to rule over many. But even greater is God's wonderful grace and his gift of righteousness, for all who receive it will live in triumph over sin and death through this one man, Jesus Christ" (Romans 5:17 NLT).

Basically, this says that through the sins of Adam and Eve, all of humanity has the desire to act in a sinful way. Because of Adam, who willfully sinned after his wife was deceived into sinning, a separation between God and humanity took place, physically and spiritually. But Jesus, being fully God and fully human, was able to right the wrongs of Adam, bringing us back to God. Because of His wonderful grace and His payment for our sins, those of us who believe in and follow Jesus as our Savior get to overcome sin and death, not be enslaved by them. Not only does He empower us to overcome sin; He also went through His fair share of trials, tribulations, and even temptations.

Jesus' temptation by Satan represents one of the most significant events revealing Jesus' humanity. Luke and Matthew detail the Holy Spirit leading Jesus from His baptism into the wilderness (Matthew 4:1; Luke 4:1). He did not lead Jesus to an oasis, a private getaway, or some inner self-discovery retreat. No, the Spirit of God led Jesus into a place of *temptation* by the devil (Matthew 4:1). But why? Don't we specifically pray for God not to lead us into temptation in the Lord's Prayer (Matthew 6:13)? This seems counter to what Christ shows us to pray to God.

James 1:13 assures us that God in no way tempts us to sin; that is strictly the workings of the Enemy. Being the tempter he is, Satan is bound to show up at any given point in time and present us with an alternative to God's call and instruction to us. God allows temptation because He has given us free will. He created us with the right to choose whether we listen to and obey Him or give in to the Enemy's temptations. But God does not leave us to succumb to our fleshly desires, vulnerable and weak, with no hope of overcoming. The Lord's Prayer indicates we can call upon God to deliver us from temptations and put a stop to the Evil One's plans. God will never lead us into sin, but when we inevitably face Satan's snares, the Lord faithfully leads us out of temptation and empowers us to resist his schemes. Okay, now that I'm done with that theological soapbox, let's get back to Jesus, shall we?

Over forty days, the devil tempted Jesus in three specific ways. Did Jesus overcome the tempter? Yes, every single time. But do you think that was easy on Jesus? For forty days, Jesus fasted in the wilderness (ate no food) and underwent ruthless attacks from the Enemy. I have fasted in the past, and even during short periods of time without food, I become irritable, more susceptible to misjudgment, more enticed by food, and overall more vulnerable. To imagine doing that for forty days . . . in the Israeli wilderness . . . with Satan badgering me 24/7 . . . and no food in my system? Jesus really went through it, friend! Not only do I feel for Jesus; He feels for us. He endured the hardest of circumstances and resisted all the way to the cross so He could give us the freedom we need to overcome sin.

Satisfying Our Appetites

When Christ had every attack waging war against Him during His temptation, what did He do? He relied on the truth of the Father and the Scriptures to sustain Him against the lies and deceptive tactics of Satan. Whenever Satan tried to get Jesus to question His identity, doubt the truth, and give in to his schemes, Jesus always relied on reciting and remembering the truth of Scripture. This is really interesting, because Jesus Himself is the Word of God spoken into being. John 1:1 and John 1:14 show Him as the walking Word, the Word made flesh, God incarnate! His life aligned with Scripture because He was God in human form. Christ also calls Himself the Bread of Life in John 6:35. When we read Scripture and spend time with Jesus, we get our daily bread; He is the spiritual portion that satisfies our appetite, cravings, and hunger.

Like I said earlier, when I haven't eaten, I become more vulnerable and susceptible to consume whatever seems pleasing and gratifying in the moment. In the same way, when we wait long periods of time without nourishment from God's Word and quality time with Jesus, our hunger steers us to meet our needs with whatever is convenient and instant. Satan is always hiding around the corner, ready to waft enticing remedies our way, but if we're full on the Bread of Life, those insatiable desires will dwindle as we develop an appetite for what is real. For the truth. Psalm 145:16, 19 says, "You open your hand; you satisfy the desire of every living thing . . . He fulfills the desire of those who fear him; he also hears their cry and saves them" (ESV). Jesus went through temptation, overcame it, and gave us a strategy to navigate it: knowing the truth, and believing it to be true. That is our escape route! That is where we will satisfy our appetite! That is what our human heart truly craves!

He Went Through It to Free You from It

He went through trials of temptation yet overcame.

He went through grief and suffering yet overcame.

He went through crucifixion and death yet overcame.

For *you*. To know you, and to love you, and to save you. Jesus did not live a glamorous life, or one free from trials, suffering, or the realities of this world. Jesus was rejected by His people and criticized by the religious leaders. He was beaten, mocked, scorned, and humiliated, then betrayed and killed in the most brutal way. He lived among humans as a human, so He could relate to us in our suffering and so that we could share in His victory.

It's surprisingly easy to overlook all that Jesus did for us. It's easy to just read it and assume it was easy for Him. Was it? No. But it was worth it. To Him, you were worth *everything*. He lived a perfect life and died a sinner's death so He could know you and love you. Matthew 20:28 says, "For even the Son of Man came not to be served but to serve others and to give his life as a ransom for many" (NLT). Friend, if anybody gets what you feel and what you are enduring, it's Jesus. He knows how tricky Satan is and how he dangles temptations before us. He knows how we so easily rationalize and romanticize poor decisions and live to regret them. Look at the disciples, the imperfect men He did life with. He knows about flaky friends and wicked enemies. He gets us, fully. He created us and knows our innermost being, just like Psalm 139:13 says.

FRIEND, IF ANYBODY GETS WHAT YOU FEEL AND WHAT YOU ARE ENDURING, IT'S JESUS.

Jesus is fully divine but was also human for our sake, so that we can be free and have a relationship with our Creator. He is our Savior, our Messiah, our hope! Praise God for Jesus, because He came for us: the lost, broken, hopeless, exhausted, confused, doubting sinners, for the sick, the saints, the hungry *humans*. He knows us best and knows we need Him when we are tempted, tired, anxious, and overwhelmed, when we have cravings only He can satisfy. He will show up every single time we call on His name for help in our humanity. He will not shy away from pulling you out of that pit you're in or meeting you in the wilderness where you're wandering. The devil talks the talk, but Jesus will show you how to walk the walk of victory.

BATTLE PLAN STEP #5:
Know Yourself

As we understand our enemy, our beloved Jesus, and our human selves more, we can accurately and tactically target the areas where Satan tempts, steals, distances, and isolates us in our walk with Jesus. Let's revisit some key points about our humanity we need to remember as we ready ourselves to address our sin:

- We are not superhuman or subhuman; we are human! God created and understands the intricate parts of us, including our free will, struggles, desires, and yearning to live life as He meant it.
- We are not perfect, but Jesus is. He was superhuman, fully God and fully man. That was how He could live a perfect life, pay for our sins by His death on the cross, and overcome it all through resurrection power. Since He is our Savior, we get to share in His victory.
- We are not alone in this. Jesus 100% understands what we are going through, how we think, what we feel, and how hard it can be to resist temptation. He did not withhold Himself from the human experience, so He can relate to us and we can rely on Him, the One who overcame Satan. He wants us to call upon His name and reach out to Him in times of trouble and temptation. He will always provide a way of escape for us.
- We are not able to overcome temptations and stop sinning by our own strength but by the power of the gospel and the truth of Scripture. When we spend time in God's Word and with Christ, He not only gives us perspective and a desire to do good; He satisfies any craving we have with the real thing, not the counterfeits Satan proposes to us.

CHAPTER SEVEN

NOT MY WILLPOWER, BUT HIS WILL BE DONE

After nine long years of suffering from chronic migraines, I decided to see if I could do anything to prevent them holistically rather than popping a pill to drown out the pain. Those pills alleviated the symptoms, but I wanted to get to the root cause and see if I could find any triggers stirred up by fragrances, chemicals, and, most importantly, food. I began reading loads of books that dove into the details of health, wellness, and nutrition, hoping to find the cause of my migraines and nourish my body better overall. Although I did find a few studies and tips for foods to avoid and those to incorporate more into my diet, one book surprised me most. While flipping through pages and highlighting phrases in Susan Peirce Thompson's book *Bright Line Eating*, I came across an incredible statement about willpower and its link to temptation.

Thompson is not just a candid author with a PhD and valuable insight into nutrition and the human brain, but she has also battled addictions to food and substances. Her book helps people take charge of their eating addictions, disorders, and bad habits. A friend of mine recommended it to me when I told her I wanted to see if added sugars were triggering my migraines. I ended up learning so much more than I expected about our body and brain's link to addiction and temptation, and I want to share some of that insight.

She wrote,

> We often think of willpower as an aspect of our moral character, or as a tool that gets more effective with increased commitment. . . . Willpower is a simple brain function. And while studies have shown that there is a genetic component to how strong it is, there is a lot more to it than genes. It's important to understand that willpower is not merely a mental faculty that resists temptation—it also governs other things, like the ability to focus. It monitors our task performance, regulates our emotions, and, most important, helps us make choices.[1]

Susan shares how she bridged the willpower gap in her life and in the lives of her clients. She focused on the lack of willpower available to us emotionally after a long day of choices and responsibilities. I know for me, I felt weakest in my battle against lust at the end of the day. By evening, after exerting willpower all day, I became tired and vulnerable, and I found it much easier to give in to what I didn't want to do. Perhaps you relate to this. If you do, know that millions of others do too! The studies speak for themselves.

Susan writes about wanting to help people move from putting pressure on the part of the brain involved in willpower, the prefrontal cortex, to the *automatic* part of their brain where the basal ganglia reside. I know, I know. This sounds like a science class. Trust me, science was my least favorite subject in school, but God created our bodies so intricately and intentionally, and understanding this in light of our temptations and inclinations will help you not only resist temptation but *rid* yourself of it!

Obedience on Autopilot

How long does a sinful action need to be repeated to develop into a hellish habit? Susan refers to a habit as an *automatic* behavior. She went into further detail, writing,

> The brain evolved to make certain behaviors automatic; this frees up other parts of the brain for making decisions . . . The basal ganglia is the part of the brain responsible for [making behaviors automatic]. . . . How long does it take for us to form a new habit? Researchers wanted to know, so they asked subjects to start a new eating, drinking, or activity behavior and record whether they carried out the behavior each day, and whether it felt

automatic to do it. On average, it took 66 days for the new behavior to become 95 percent automatic.[2]

It takes sixty-six days to form a new habit and establish it as an *automatic* action. This is interesting to me because within that timeframe, you could read one book of the Bible every day and finish the whole Bible! What sticks out to me, though, is that our centers for *decision-making* and for *automaticity* reside in different parts of our brain. For some of us, the sin that binds us doesn't require a decision; it feels automatic! It's like that sin gets programmed in us, and we try to eradicate the virus that's overriding our system. However, when we try to exert our willpower alone, we get burned out and short-circuit, and our hopes of moving forward dissipate again. Fear not, my friend. There are two important truths I want you to know.

> IT TAKES SIXTY-SIX DAYS TO FORM A NEW HABIT AND ESTABLISH IT AS AN *AUTOMATIC* ACTION.

Rely on His Strength

First, we do not have to rely on our own willpower. We get to rely on *God's* power. Matthew 26:41 says, "Watch and pray so that you will not fall into temptation. The spirit is willing, but the flesh is weak." Read that again: The spirit is *willing*, but the flesh is *weak*. Our spirit, our being, once exposed to the goodness of

God, desires to do what is right, honorable, and obedient. Our spirit is indeed willing. However, the flesh—our carnal nature and its appetites—is weak and susceptible to being swayed by the comforts and counterfeits we've previously settled for. Luckily, we are not alone, nor do we have to rely on our own strength to overcome.

The Word is our weapon (Ephesians 6:17), prayer is a weapon (Ephesians 6:18), our faith and trust in God and His truth is a weapon (1 Peter 5:8–9), and our submission to God is a weapon against the Evil One (James 4:7). God promises this: "No temptation has overtaken you except what is common to mankind. And God is faithful; he will not let you be tempted beyond what you can bear. But when you are tempted, he will also provide a way out so that you can endure it" (1 Corinthians 10:13). When we begin to do life with Christ and submit to Him as Lord, He gives us the gift of the Holy Spirit to help us (John 16:7). When the Holy Spirit takes root in your life, and you actively abide with Him and by Him (1 John 4:13), He begins to produce fruit in your life (Galatians 5:22–23). You know one of the fruits He produces? Self-control. Another word for willpower. He will produce within and for you the divine self-control needed to resist and press on as you remain close to Christ and His call for you.

I don't know if you've ever been in an expert-level escape room, but the trials you're facing and the temptations you are enduring are not like that. God is not orchestrating difficult puzzles to solve like some wicked game master who wants to see if you'll escape in time. No. On the contrary, He holds the door wide open and plasters a huge neon exit sign right above it. He points you away from sin and toward freedom when temptation shows its face.

"Lord, how do I get out of this room of lust and sexual sin?" *Walk out of the room, change your environment, turn on some worship music, read John 15, and let Me strengthen you to resist temptation with the truth!*

"God, how do I escape from comparison and sabotaging others?" *Take a step back from your surroundings, spend time in Romans 12 and 1 Corinthians 12, then allow Me to remind you of your identity and unique calling as well as theirs, because you both matter greatly to Me!*

"Father, I am so easily influenced around these friends to act out in rebellion. I swear, drink, and get high every time we hang out. How do I change?" *Step out of that friend group; remember who I've created you to be and the fullness of life I have for you outside of rebellion; accept My correction and conviction; rely on My strength in temptation; and share My words with your friends instead!*

WE NEED TO MAKE A PRACTICE OF CALLING UPON THE NAME OF JESUS IN THOSE MOMENTS WHEN WE MOST WANT TO RUN INTO THE ARMS OF SIN.

Friend, you and I both need to rely on God. We must take a step back and allow God to step in. We need to accept what He corrects and see the love behind everything He says and does. We need to make a practice of calling upon the name of Jesus in those moments when we most want to run into the arms of sin. The Lord will give you strength to endure, and although it may be causing you pressure right now, this little while longer of *going* through will only reveal in time what God was *growing* you through.

One Change at a Time

Second, we do not have to exhaust ourselves trying to make a million right decisions. Instead, we can establish one right routine. Let's think about what a habit is. It is something we do automatically, revert back to, our "factory setting" if you will. When you get knocked down by the Enemy or when you've had a bad day, what is your default setting? For some of us, it is getting in God's presence and filling ourselves with Scripture. For many of us, though, sin offers the place where we've found the most comfort for coping and de-stressing. A habit is not just something we do repeatedly; it is an automatic behavior. My hope for you, and that I imagine you have for yourself, is to create *holy habits* that surface on the days when you're tired and exhausted. May *those* become your comfort and default when your willpower has run out. This is the automaticity Susan referred to.

When I set up routines in my life, certain actions automatically follow. For instance, I wake up in the morning, brush my teeth, wash my face, and put on my skincare for the day. Then I either give my husband a quick cuddle and kiss before heading to my workout class or start my quiet time with God. Over the past few years of marriage, this has been my routine, instilling in me an automatic response from the second my alarm goes off. How did it become automatic, though?

For routines to develop into automatic responses rather than a series of active choices, it takes time, discipline, and repetition. I know we live in a day and age where we want instant results and immediate fixes, but if you're going to get free, you have to understand that discipline is a process that takes time (like sanctification) along with repetition, enforcing your choices over and over again. Bodybuilders don't become bodybuilders overnight. They show up every day and practice to prepare for competition day. They live by a specific diet, a specific workout, a specific daily lifestyle that leads to results. Discipline is the product of patience and practice, but it also requires boundaries and routine.

Freedom in Action!

Maybe this all seems overwhelming to you.

If that's how you feel right now, I don't blame you!

If we look at the place and person we want to be compared to where we are stuck right now and who we are today, it can feel discouraging and impossible. I promise you this isn't wishful thinking. It wasn't for me when I was in the thick of my porn addiction, because today I am writing to you as a free woman! I don't want you to compare where you are right now to where you will be. You will get there because He will get you there. In the meantime, just focus on where you are *today* and what you want to accomplish *tomorrow*.

> SMALL STEPS MAKE UP BIG STRIDES, AND OVER TIME, YOU WILL BE ABLE TO LOOK BACK AND SEE JUST HOW FAR YOU'VE COME.

Small steps make up big strides, and over time, you will be able to look back and see just how far you've come. Take it one day at a time and embrace the new mercies God has for you every day.

When I make plans, I see better results. When I plan out my

day the night before, I get more checked off my list because I have already taken time to make decisions and think things through. When I plan out my meals for the week, I don't order in food every night, and my wallet thanks me. When I plan my outfit the evening before church, my husband is a happy man who doesn't have to wait on me in the car for "just a second." It's smooth sailing when I plan ahead, and I did the same thing with my sin. I formed a plan of action so that when I was vulnerable and had no more willpower to give, I had something to rely on. With patience and practice, that became a habit—a holy habit!

Here was my action plan: If I felt vulnerable and susceptible to sinning with pornography, I would leave all my electronics in one room, step out of that room, tell someone I was struggling and needed prayer, and read out loud a list of Scripture and truth-claims over myself, about my God, and against the Enemy. Sometimes I would even do this while jumping around or walking outside just to get my body moving. It felt silly at first, but who cares about silly when your freedom is on the line, when addiction is ruining your life, and you are drowning in self-hatred and hopelessness? I made a practice of this, and as I repeated it over and over again, it became easier to resist the Enemy and substitute his temptations with holy habits that empowered me to walk out freedom.

I want you to make an action plan of your own. It could be exactly like mine for the exact same sin, or it could be tailored specifically to the sin or situation you need freedom from. Whatever it looks like, share it with someone and put that thing into action. As we get into a rhythm of repeating holy actions daily with well-thought-out and preplanned options, it will build the muscle of our willpower. We won't crumble under pressure when sinful habits sneak up and tempt us because we've already mapped out a plan regarding that thought, that impulse, that idea. Preplanning, practice, and patience will cultivate the discipline that leads to freedom.

Red Light, Green Light

Routines help us set up what I call *green-light zones* and *red-light zones*. Scrolling on social media first thing in the morning falls in the red-light zone for me, because I will literally lie in bed for who knows how long if I do that first thing. I've stuck to my established routine with planning, preparation, and practice, so my automatic response changed; I no longer waste time in bed when I know I have things to do. I get up, get ready for the day, make my pre-workout energy drink, and head to my workout class, listening to worship music the entire way there. That always leads to me feeling accomplished and ready for my day. I have time and space for scrolling and phone time *after* my routine; then it falls in the green-light zone.

Some things perpetually belong in the red-light zone: they are a no-go. For instance, when I was really wrestling with porn in college, phone use past a certain time at night was in my red-light zone. I even deleted certain apps from my phone; they're perpetually in the red-light zone because that boundary provides safety and security to me and honor to the Lord.

Are you green-lighting anything in your life that is actually harmful and should be red-lighted? Maybe you need to red-light it until you instill some routine and discipline in your life, to avoid exhausting your willpower and instead make wise choices.

I encourage you to even talk about possible obstacles with your mentor, pastor, trusted leader, or your community to see if they have any insight. It won't be easy, but defining clear boundaries with activities in the green-light and red-light zones will free you from decisions that could make a wreck of your life.

Set Your Green-Light and Red-Light Zones

Sin has undoubtedly overstayed its welcome in our lives. How do we kick it out and put an end to the automatic responses we run back to in moments of weakness, hurt, or when our rhythms are attacked by the Enemy? Let's summarize all we just learned about redeeming our repetitive inclinations and setting up boundaries and disciplines:

- Identify your struggles. Determine weak points in your life where you keep making allowances and have a hard time denying impulses.
- Rely on God's power instead of your own willpower and strength alone. When you call upon the name of Jesus, walk with His Holy Spirit in day-to-day life, and let His truth take deep root in your heart, self-control and new desires will naturally spring forth and empower you to resist once repetitive sins.
- Implement new routines and boundaries into your life and plan out your next steps before you run into temptation. By preparing an action plan ahead of time, you can default to a better response than if you were to have no strategy for battle against the Enemy.
- Start by making changes in just one area of your life. By implementing routines, battle plans, and boundaries ahead

of time in one area, these repeated actions will become automatic. Automatic obedience and freedom will replace automatic sin.

- Establish red-light and green-light zone activities. By clearly marking what is sinful, nonnegotiable, and/or harmful toward your health and healing, you can begin to eliminate actions, thoughts, and patterns that lead you into areas of collision.

CHAPTER EIGHT

CONFESSING AND REPENTING WHAT'S BEEN KEPT IN

What if I told you I stole a diamond bracelet worth thousands of dollars from a jewelry store when I was four years old? Yeah, I was basically the inspiration behind *Ocean's Eight*. To be fair, it was my nana Marsha's store, and she told me I could have the bracelet one day (lies—I never received it). I didn't believe she would actually save it for me (I was correct, but maybe that's because I stole it). It was so shiny, so big, so beautiful. So when nobody was looking, I snatched it from the display rack, threw it into my Tinker Bell suitcase, and walked out the back of the store where I knew I wouldn't set off the alarms. I was four—how did I even know that?

As the day went on, I felt kind of bad for what I'd done—for going behind my nana's back and taking something that didn't belong to me . . . yet. I tried to ignore that feeling of guilt and act like nothing even happened. Later that evening, after my bath, I walked into my grandparents' bedroom where my brother and I were staying, and there was my mom. Standing there. Holding the diamond bracelet. I quickly shot a glance at my Tinker Bell suitcase. She had opened it and found it in there. My eyes shot back to my mom. She asked me bluntly, "Kirby, did you steal this from Nana Marsha's store?" She was shocked that her little Kirby had embraced a life of crime. I stared at her wide-eyed, eventually nodding my head yes. "You need to confess to her what you did and return this to her," she commanded me. She handed me the bracelet, and I took the long journey in my Cinderella nightgown down to my nana in the kitchen.

"Nana Marsha?" I quietly called. She saw me standing there with tears welling up in my eyes. She looked at me with concern, only to notice the huge diamond bracelet dangling in my tiny hands. "I took the bracelet. I'm so sorry," I wept. She came over to me, hugged me, took back the bracelet, and forgave me. I explained to her why I stole it, how sorry I was, and that I would never steal ever again. The humiliation of getting caught was enough of a lesson to never steal ever again . . . Okay, I confess, I did steal a lollipop from the corner store when I was eight, but that's it . . . Okay, and my mom's credit card information to buy music for my iPod when I was twelve—*now* that's it! My days of crime are over, and even as I look back at that memory and laugh about how on earth I nearly got away with it, I learned that through confession, I was able to experience freedom from guilt and reconciliation in relationships that mattered most to me.

A juvenile example, I know, but whether you're a four-year-old felon like me or are wrestling with a habitual sin, confession is not easy. To humble ourselves and admit we are wrong makes us very vulnerable. Regardless of whether it is a sin against yourself or someone else, we can dread admitting guilt and confessing our mistakes. Personally, I hate to let people down. It's hard to own the fault and accept the outcome. However, when we initiate confession and allow what is in the darkness to come into the light, we begin to see the clear path and direction God calls us to as we walk out repentance. Confession kicks off great new beginnings, where we walk as new creations.

> WHEN WE INITIATE CONFESSION AND ALLOW WHAT IS IN THE DARKNESS TO COME INTO THE LIGHT, WE BEGIN TO SEE THE CLEAR PATH AND DIRECTION GOD CALLS US TO AS WE WALK OUT REPENTANCE.

Whatever burden weighs you down, and whatever corner you've tried to stuff your sin and shame into, this is the time and place to lay it all out. You don't have to keep hiding it, fighting it, fearing it, or hearing it taunt you, keeping you stagnant. As followers of Christ, we are called to go and to run—not to remain in the darkness but to walk in the light (John 12:46–47; Romans 13:12) and bring light to the world (Matthew 5:14–16). That has to start with us, with confession.

Confession is not just an admission of fault; it also calls for *renouncing* sin. When we confess and renounce, we find mercy. That is the order found in Proverbs 28:13. "Whoever conceals their sins does not prosper, but the one who confesses and renounces them finds mercy." To renounce an old way of living, thinking, believing, or behaving is to literally "disown," "deny," "cast off," or "reject."[1] When we renounce an old way of living and leading our lives, we aren't just saying, *I won't do it again*, but completely disowning and rejecting that behavior. We are saying, *That is no longer who I am and what I'm about.*

Confession opens the door to receiving mercy, the most bountiful and beautiful measure of God's love for us. Lamentations 3:22–23 says, "The steadfast love of the LORD never ceases; his mercies never come to an end; they are new every morning; great is your faithfulness" (ESV). God's patient love never stops running after us, never stops looking for us. In His love, He extends mercy to us every day, meaning that we *do not* get what we once *deserved*: judgment for our sins. Because of mercy, God withholds that verdict from us. Instead, through grace, *giving* us what we *don't deserve*, we receive the righteousness of Christ to stand before Him, forgiven and purified from what once contaminated us. He faithfully meets us with mercy and grace every day, every time we fall short in our sins.

Who Do We Confess To?

God instructs us to confess our sins to Him and our Christian community. You need to find people you can be real with, who you trust, and who genuinely care for your well-being. But first and foremost, confess your sins to the Lord. Only by confessing can you experience forgiveness and the joy found in it.

Psalm 32:3 says, "For when I kept silent, my bones wasted away through my groaning all day long" (ESV). Whenever I was living in active sin, afraid to approach God and confess my actions as wrong, that was exactly how it felt—like my bones were wasting away and groaning. I could feel the disturbance in my soul, a lack of peace, and anxiety so great the butterflies in my stomach felt like bats. Friend, you do not need to fear coming before God and acknowledging your bad choices. He loves you, He wants to forgive you, and He will give you healing as you pursue a life of freedom with Him. If you no longer want to feel like your heart and soul are dwindling and defeated, your groaning needs to shift to owning your disobedience. You need to acknowledge it as a sin against God. Only when we admit our shortcomings can we move on toward forgiveness, freedom, sanctification, and maturity in our faith.

Scripture also encourages us to acknowledge our sins to others so we can be healed. Jesus' brother James wrote, "Therefore confess your sins to each other and pray for each other so that you may be healed. The prayer of a righteous person is powerful and effective" (James 5:16). When we confess our sins to community, friends, mentors, and leaders who are also Christians, we not only get to experience healing but also have the opportunity to be ministered to, prayed for, loved, encouraged, seen, and surrounded when we need help and support.

Together Is Better and Biblical!

You and I were never meant to do life alone. We need authentic community who will show up when we are weak, who speak life and identity over us when our sin seems impossible to conquer. When I confessed my sin of porn to a friend, it brought me freedom as she prayed and ministered over me. Confession to others is not meant to shame you. I know we might believe that lie, or perhaps we have been shamed in the past by an unhealthy community we once trusted, but my hope for you is that God highlights at least one person who can walk alongside you as you bring sin from the dark into the light.

Confessing our sins and surrounding ourselves with prayer brings healing, power, and freedom to our lives. I am proof of that! And you know what? I continued to reach out to my community to pray for me and surround me with truth, accountability, and encouragement as I started to walk in freedom with more boldness and transparency. The more I brought my sin into the light and allowed trusted people to know my struggles, the more empowered I felt to walk out repentance and release what was destroying me. The Enemy wants to isolate and shame you in your sin. He does not want you to win. He knows that when you open your mouth, admit where you've been struggling, and commit to change, God will begin the good work of releasing you from the previous desires and ways you lived.

CONFESSION IS A CATALYST THAT WILL EMPOWER YOU TO BE FREE.

Confession leads to change, healing, and stronger community. It leads to deeper trust and reliance on God. It doesn't blame, shame, belittle, or disqualify you. Confession is a catalyst that will empower you to be free.

He Is Faithful and Just to Forgive Us

We chatted earlier about the lies we believe about God. They warp our perception of loving, knowing, and approaching God with confidence in our confessions. Satan does a good job of getting us to see God incorrectly, but he isn't the only one; other people also influence our relationship with God and whether we reach out to Him or retreat from Him when we mess up. Perhaps you project bad examples of authority or fatherhood onto God because of how others have misled, abused, or manipulated you. As someone with an imperfect father, I am so sorry you had to endure that, but your dad is not God. God will not treat you as imperfect people do, because He is good, loving, and perfect. He doesn't hold grudges; He shows us forgiveness and helps us to move forward. He blots our sin out entirely (Isaiah 43:25).

It's a simple gospel, friend. God forgives! First John 1:9 declares, "If we confess our sins, he is faithful and just and will forgive us our sins and purify us from all unrighteousness." His Word is truth, which means this verse is true for you too. When we confess our sins and choose to do things God's way, He is *faithful* to forgive us and is *fair* in forgiving us. Even though we might feel undeserving or like it doesn't make any sense, it makes all the sense in the world as we understand Christ's work on the cross. When we put our faith in Him and choose to make Him the Lord of our life, Jesus takes on our sin, shame, mistakes, and mess-ups, and exchanges these for justification, righteousness, and a clean record before God. We can fairly and fully

WHEN WE CONFESS OUR SINS AND CHOOSE TO DO THINGS GOD'S WAY, HE IS *FAITHFUL* TO FORGIVE US AND IS *FAIR* IN FORGIVING US.

be forgiven because of what Jesus did and who He is. God cannot and will not go back on His Word. His mercy and forgiveness are just like Him: eternally faithful.

Walking in the Will of God

Confession is an admission, but *repentance* is the action that follows. That's another fancy church word we hear on Sundays. To *repent* means that you decide, through a change of mind and heart, to turn in the opposite direction from where you were once wandering and start walking in the will and ways of God. It is the narrow path, the road of obedience, the holy highway. We don't just want to talk the talk and confess. We also need to walk the walk and repent.

> WE DON'T JUST WANT TO TALK THE TALK AND CONFESS. WE ALSO NEED TO WALK THE WALK AND REPENT.

If you are familiar with the Gospels (the first four books of the New Testament that detail Jesus' life and ministry), then you are probably aware of Jesus' disciple Peter. Peter was just an average, everyday Galilean fisherman. He was an impulsive man who often spoke whatever came to mind, was assertive and temperamental at times, and desired to do right even though he messed up quite a bit. He was simply human, like you and me. A significant part of Peter's story occurred on the night of Jesus' betrayal. When Jesus was arrested and tried before the Sanhedrin and other religious lawmakers of His region (unlawfully, I might add), Peter denied being His close friend and follower three times (Matthew 26:69–75; Luke 22:54–62), even though he had said he would never deny Him (Matthew 26:33–35). Peter made a promise to Jesus with good intentions but failed to follow through. I relate, Peter; I relate. Hours later, Jesus was crucified on the cross, leaving His disciples in utter distress. But the story for Jesus and Peter didn't end there.

Three days later, Jesus overcame death and conquered our sin, leaving it behind on the cross and in the grave. Some time passed before the resurrected Jesus met Peter again. What do you think Jesus did the second He saw Peter, one of His best friends who had rejected Him in His greatest hour of need? Did He tell Peter off? Did He refuse to make eye contact with him until he groveled and begged for Jesus' pity? Did He banish Peter for being a bad friend who didn't keep his word? Did He revoke Peter's salvation and cast him aside to be tormented by the Enemy? No. Jesus *redeemed* Peter. He delivered and pardoned him, meeting Peter with grace, understanding, and compassion. In fact, He still chose to love Peter and use him for great plans and purposes despite his downfall. That is the heart of God, friend: redemption, restoration, and reconciliation.

Redemption is "the release of people, animals, or property from bondage through the payment of a price."[2] *Restoration* "denotes giving or receiving something back that was taken or lost."[3] *Reconciliation* is the "restoration of friendly relationships and of peace where there had previously been hostility and alienation. Ordinarily, it also includes the removal of the offense that caused the disruption of peace and harmony."[4] When Peter recognized what he had done wrong and returned to Jesus with a repentant heart, Jesus was faithful to forgive, restore, and continue in relationship with him.

Peter went on to do amazing things for the gospel, preaching boldly to crowds about Jesus the Messiah, his Savior and friend. He even wrote two books in the New Testament: 1 and 2 Peter. In 2 Peter 3:9, he wrote, "The Lord is not slow about his promise, as some think of slowness, but is patient with you, not wanting any to perish, but all to come to repentance" (NRSV). Peter was not just writing this to write it, or only because the Holy Spirit inspired him to do so. He also *knew* this truth in his experience of walking with the living God. *Peter* wrote this. Please realize that! Our God is patient, wanting us to repent and draw near to be reconciled, walking in freedom and fullness.

We've All Made Mistakes

We often hold the misconception that people in Scripture were the holiest of the holy and never did any wrong; that must be why God chose them. Did you ever stop to think that in the grand narrative of the Bible and in all its history and revelation, these were the lives of *real* people that we are reading about? People who struggled with lust, pride, envy, doubt, greed, gossip, faithlessness, addiction, temptation, and every other sin.

Take David, for example, the guy God called "a man after his own heart" (1 Samuel 13:14). Many Christians look up to David as a hero, an example, a person they aspire to be like. He was all that, but he was also the guy who assassinated a woman's husband just so he could cover up the fact that he had sex with her and got her pregnant. That's right. David was the God-fearing, humble shepherd boy but was also the lying, lustful murderer. But God knew what he did. He sent the prophet Nathan to call David out in front of everyone. Can you imagine? Your deepest, darkest secret on display in front of everyone who looked up to you?

Your image, shattered.

Your illusions, destroyed.

Your biggest insecurities, revealed.

If that were me, I would either die from embarrassment or run away as far as I could, like Adam and Eve when they hid themselves from God. But what did David do with his sin, on display for all to see? Psalm 51 records David's response to his conviction. Rather than running away from God, abandoning his identity as God's child and his call as a servant and king, he responded by running *toward* God and repenting.

I am so grateful that the Bible does not leave out the ugly, messy, real, and raw moments of humanity. It just goes to show how desperately we need a Savior, and how, apart from God, we are depraved. We need His help, forgiveness, love, correction, and power at work within us to transform us into His likeness. God preserved these stories in His living Word to reveal humanity's nature and His own as well.

Now, I've never lusted after another person's husband, killed his wife, then forced him to marry me like David with Bathsheba and Uriah, but I have had my sin exposed and felt the weight of shame and embarrassment from it. I've seen that happen to friends and family as well, where their deepest, darkest sinful habits were revealed before others, and they felt utterly humiliated. That feeling makes you want to curl up in a ball under the covers of your bed, never to see the light of day again. Maybe that's how David felt too. But his story gives us hope because, in the vulnerable, harsh reality of how far we can fall, we are shown the triumphant truth that God always welcomes us back through repentance. *Always.*

IN THE VULNERABLE, HARSH REALITY OF HOW FAR WE CAN FALL, WE ARE SHOWN THE TRIUMPHANT TRUTH THAT GOD ALWAYS WELCOMES US BACK THROUGH REPENTANCE.

Return to Your Redeemer

Repentance in Greek, *metanoia*, literally means to change one's mind. But it's more than just our thoughts; it is a conscious redirection toward something completely different. It requires an acknowledgment of what we did, where we were heading, what we believed, where we went wrong, and a choice to change our ways—not just behaviorally but our thoughts, convictions, and direction. This was the heart of the gospel, the good news, that Jesus came to preach. "From then on Jesus began to preach, 'Repent of your sins and turn to God, for the Kingdom of Heaven is near'" (Matthew 4:17 NLT).

The Lord says in Isaiah 44:22, "I have swept away your offenses like a cloud, your sins like the morning mist. Return to me, for I have redeemed you." This idea of returning and reorienting encompasses repentance. God cleanses us of our sins, clears our record of wrongdoing, and invites us to walk with Him in the direction of His plans and purposes. I love that when we repent, we don't have to complete specific tasks or rituals to make ourselves right before God. Trust me, I have fallen into this way of thinking, believing that I have to do certain things to get right with God again and pay off the debt of my sin; but that is not the gospel. My works don't save me; Jesus' work saves me! Christ's payment on the cross for our sins cancels our debt and justifies us before God in full.

GOD CLEANSES US OF OUR SINS, CLEARS OUR RECORD OF WRONGDOING, AND INVITES US TO WALK WITH HIM IN THE DIRECTION OF HIS PLANS AND PURPOSES.

Jesus paid it *all*. Every ounce of blood He shed purifies us before God. By His grace and mercy we can turn away from our sins and move forward in the direction God is calling us toward—a radical relationship with Him. We don't have to stress about earning a place at His table.

A Seat with Your Name on It

Have you ever been to a party, a dinner, or an event where you felt like you didn't fit in with the rest of the crowd—like they were so much better than you or more deserving to be invited? My husband and I were invited to a huge gala in Washington, DC, for a Christian organization where hundreds of people showed up—my ministry heroes, CEOs, and people I'd never normally sit at a table with. But there I was. And it wasn't because of anything I had done to earn a spot there; it was because the host invited me. I had just as much right to be there as anyone else because the event coordinator had prepared a place for me. There was a seat with my name on it.

The same goes for our relationship with Christ. Just because you aren't a super-Christian who avoids falling repeatedly into the same sin, an original apostle who walked hand in hand with Jesus, a celebrity pastor, or a world-renowned theologian doesn't mean you don't belong at Christ's table. He is inviting you to sit, break bread, and have a relationship with Him because He wants you there, not because of anything you have or haven't done. Our belief in Christ and faithfulness to follow Him are enough. The admission of your need for a Savior and your submission to Him as Lord of your life takes care of every single mistake you have made. I mean, look at David! If there is hope for him—a murderous, covetous, lustful liar—then there is hope for you and me. You know why? Because God did not see him as that. He saw David as a redeemed, beloved, forgiven human. Underneath all David had done, God knew the true treasure in David's heart and the real identity that could rise from the ashes of his sin. We will also be met with grace and forgiveness when we choose to turn from our rebellion and reorient our hearts and lives toward the will and ways of God. This has always been true for humanity and our loving God.

The Pain We May Have Caused

Hear me loud and clear: *God forgave David.* He also forgave Noah, Abraham, Peter, Paul, and so many others we place on pedestals. Yes, these are the heroes of the faith, but really, they were honest-to-God *humans.* If God forgave them, He will forgive you too. We can have hope in that promise because God does not change (Malachi 3:6).

Alongside our repentance and reconciliation with God, we must acknowledge how our sin has hurt others. Sometimes our habitual sins oppose God alone, and other times they affect those around us. It is hard and humbling to acknowledge the pain we might have caused others, but God helps to heal and reconcile what needs to be restored. Other times,

> IT IS HARD AND HUMBLING TO ACKNOWLEDGE THE PAIN WE MIGHT HAVE CAUSED OTHERS, BUT GOD HELPS TO HEAL AND RECONCILE WHAT NEEDS TO BE RESTORED.

our sin requires some distance between us and the one we've hurt, and we have to trust that God will work to bring peace in those relationships. Regardless of whether our apologies bring about reconciliation, we can own our mistakes and honor others with genuine sorrow and take charge of our present and future choices to not repeat the cycle of hurting others. You are not a horrible person; you're a human whom God can free from painful patterns and past reputations. The character He is developing within you will speak for itself.

Your Father Will Welcome You Home

Jesus told a series of beautiful parables showcasing the Father's heart and how He feels and responds to us when we return to Him through repentance. This collection in Luke 15 includes the story of a lost sheep, a lost coin, and a lost son. Each parable, which I encourage you to read, presents a similar theme: what was lost was found. Whether the one wandering sheep sought by the shepherd who left the other ninety-nine, one of ten precious coins lost by a woman who overturned her house to find it, or the Prodigal Son who squandered his inheritance and then returned home to a welcoming father's open arms and celebration, each expresses a very important truth about God: He loves to find the lost.

In verse 6, the shepherd shouted, "Rejoice with me; I have found my lost sheep." In verse 9, the woman proclaimed, "Rejoice with me; I have found my lost coin." In verse 32, the father explained to his oldest, responsible son, "But we had to celebrate and be glad, because this brother of yours was dead and is alive again; he was lost and is found." God rejoices when *you* repent, when *you* are found, when *you* return. Jesus said, "I tell you that in the same way there will be more rejoicing in heaven over one sinner who repents than over ninety-nine righteous persons who do not need to repent" (Luke 15:7).

GOD REJOICES WHEN *YOU* REPENT, WHEN *YOU* ARE FOUND, WHEN *YOU* RETURN.

Perhaps you are under the impression that repenting and returning to God looks more like a long journey home to a Father with his arms crossed, tapping his foot in frustration, waiting at the door to give you the punishment of a lifetime. If that was how your parents treated you, I am so sorry; that may have clouded your understanding of how God handles your mistakes.

Do not be afraid to come to your Father in heaven, who loves you. From His personal sacrifice, to His continual faithfulness, to the discipline we might be shown, there is love in every ounce of it. He is the One who went through every test, trial, and obstacle to redeem and provide a way to have a loving, meaningful relationship with you. You can come home to Him, just like the Prodigal Son. He'll meet you with more grace, mercy, forgiveness, and celebration than you feel deserving of. We *are* undeserving. We are sinful and guilty. But as a just and fair judge, God looks upon Jesus' sacrifice and declares our sentence *paid in full*. Now in Christ, we are pure and blameless before Him. Make a fresh start with God; do life with Him.

BATTLE PLAN STEP #7:
Turn Around and Come Home

If you have decided to change your mind and your ways through repentance, then release the shame, the old comforts, the resentments, the regret, and the reputation that once defined you. You are no longer that person and can live pressure free! But first, let's reflect on what we just read and take time to confess and repent before the Lord:

- When we confess (admit our wrongdoings) and bring sin into the light, we begin to experience freedom, forgiveness, and healing. We need to confess our sins to God and a safe community so they can walk alongside us, help us overcome any insecurity or negative thoughts, and remind us of the truth of God's Word and love.
- When we confess, we must also repent (change our wandering direction from wickedness to God's will). Repentance involves a change of heart, mind, conviction, and desire. This was the heart of Jesus' gospel—that people would not only believe in Him but turn away from their sins and follow Him instead.
- When reading the Bible, we must remember that the real men and women in it struggled too. God knows no one is perfect, and we can see His goodness in these real and raw stories. He desires to do life with us, forgive us, and redeem us back to Him.
- When we admit our wrongdoings, we must realize that sometimes people will not accept our apologies. There will be

times when God allows reconciliation in relationships to take place, and at other times, He allows us to part ways and grow in different directions. We can trust that God can change us into new people, redeem our character, and turn our reputation into a testament of His glory and grace.

CHAPTER NINE

LET GO AND LOOK AHEAD

I know I'm not the only one who remembers a painstakingly awkward or embarrassing moment from high school in the middle of the night and does a deep dive online on everyone from school. Just me? Cool . . . totally not weird, paranoid behavior. I can get so in my head that my worst moments are thoughts of how everyone from my past remembers me. I'm sure that one girl I never really talked to only remembers me for peeing my pants from laughing too hard at my own joke in class. I'm sure that one boy I crushed on only remembers me as the girl who completely ate concrete on her skateboard the first week of school. I'm also sure one girl remembers me as a "bad friend" because her brother had a crush on me and kissed me behind her back. Some of her friends complained that I was her friend only to secretly "get with" her brother. Not true *at all*. He only kissed me to brag about it to his friends, since I was the "purity girl."

I remember crying on my mom's bed thinking my whole high school reputation was shot and my life was over. I look back now and see how juvenile that experience was, but for the longest time, I carried so much shame and felt so unworthy as a friend. I felt like I couldn't trust a guy's intentions after that either. Every time I passed that girl's friend group in the hallway, I felt so judged. A few of them were bold enough to comment the names they called me behind my back on my birthday photo I posted online. I was humiliated, full of regret, and felt so misunderstood. Eventually that girl and I reconciled, but for months I felt like I would be defined by that moment. Was this a habitual sin? No. But I'm sure you've made one-off mistakes that you are not too proud of, and you may be convinced that others will always use them to define your character.

Eventually, I had to release myself from the shame I felt from that situation. I also had to release anger toward that guy, bitterness toward those girls, and fear I had for future relationships. I've had to do that many times in various areas of my life. To release myself from the shame over my porn addiction. Hurt toward my dad for choosing another drink over his kids. Anger and resentment toward men after I was used and misled by someone I thought cared for me. Fear and people-pleasing so I could fully live out God's purposes for my life. I've been through it too, friend. I have failed, I have been hurt, I have hurt others, and I have disappointed myself. I've had to forgive others, forgive myself, and seek out forgiveness for my mistakes. I have had to acknowledge all those emotions and let go of whatever God called me to release, because you can't move freely when you're

YOU CAN'T MOVE FORWARD IF YOU'RE DWELLING ON THE PAST. YOU CAN'T HEAL AND HELP OTHERS IF YOU REFUSE TO ACKNOWLEDGE AND GROW FROM YOUR FAULTS.

stuck in bondage. You can't move forward if you're dwelling on the past. You can't heal and help others if you refuse to acknowledge and grow from your faults.

I've seen people walk in freedom, and I've seen people go to the grave limping and crawling because of their tight grip on situations and feelings they wouldn't release to God about themselves, others, and circumstances. A death grip on your past sins or the hurt from others' sins keeps you stagnant. It won't let you move on to the new season, the new stride, and the new self that God has for you. If we are going to break free from our sin, we also need to break free from shame, blame, anger, self-hatred, and anything else He convicts us to release.

Releasing What's Trapping You

Are you stuck beating yourself up about an addiction you haven't shared with anyone? Friend, release that shame.

Are you convinced you'll never be able to forgive that person for what they've done to you? Release your anger.

Are you fixated on the lie that you are solely defined by your lowest moments? Release that insecurity.

Are you believing there is no hope for your healing, that you'll fail yourself and God again and again? Release that anxiety.

Perhaps it's perfectionism, resentment, or pride. If I know one thing to be true, the Holy Spirit faithfully convicts us of the things we need to release. John 16:8 declares this: "And when he comes, he will convict the world concerning sin and righteousness and judgment" (ESV). If you allow yourself to be still in God's presence and give Him a seat at your table, He will faithfully reveal what you need to remove from your life. It's strange how sometimes we can find comfort in what we hold on to—even the attitudes and behaviors we show toward ourselves or others as a means of coping or handling our sin. But if we are going to be healed, set free, and grow deeper in our relationship with Christ, we must let go of whatever He calls us to and entrust it into His hands. This includes any ways you've been inaccurately viewing or punishing yourself. He has removed your sin far from you. He is the judge, *not you*. Psalm 103:8–14 says:

> IF YOU ALLOW YOURSELF TO BE STILL IN GOD'S PRESENCE AND GIVE HIM A SEAT AT YOUR TABLE, HE WILL FAITHFULLY REVEAL WHAT YOU NEED TO REMOVE FROM YOUR LIFE.

> The LORD is compassionate and merciful, slow to get angry and filled with unfailing love. He will not constantly accuse us, nor remain angry forever. He does not punish us for all our sins; he does not deal harshly with us, as we deserve. For his unfailing love toward those who fear him is as great as the height of the heavens above the earth. He has removed our sins as far from us as the east is from the west. The LORD is like a father to

his children, tender and compassionate to those who fear him. For he knows how weak we are; he remembers we are only dust. (NLT)

Leave the Past Behind

Shame was a huge inhibitor that kept me from fully experiencing the freedom Christ bought for me on the cross. The Lord wanted me to let certain things go so I could free my grasp to grip His call and identity for me. But shame paralyzed and crippled me when God told me I could run freely. Self-hatred and pride kept me frozen, even though the radiating love of God was warming me up to bloom and blossom in life. I felt stuck, like I couldn't go forward. Even though God had positioned me on a new path, my gaze was still fixed on the trail of past regrets. Yet they were right where they belonged—*behind me.*

So many of us live with a rear view, constantly playing back where it all went wrong, beating ourselves up for what we did. But Jesus said, "Father, forgive them, for they don't know what they are doing" (Luke 23:34 NLT). God has released you from death, punishment, and His wrath, and shows you immense grace, kindness, and new hope! Don't reject this gift He freely gives you by continuing to punish yourself for your past.

Release yourself. From that inner critic, those demonizing thoughts, that self-hatred and judgment. From false guilt or false comfort in your own sense of failure that keeps you from moving out of the past to the present, and into God's future for you. The Enemy loves to adjust our point of view to the rearview mirror instead of the road God has paved for us right ahead. Satan does all he can to shift our focus onto the sin we committed ten years, ten months, ten days, or ten minutes ago, and the result is always shame. But God does not want us to live in shame or in the past. As the famous saying goes, "There is no saint without a past, no sinner without a future."

If we are going to keep our eyes on the road, remain close to God, and move forward as He daily chips away our fleshly desires, then we must stop lingering on the past potholes we hit, the exits that rerouted us, and our pitiful pit stops. Grieve, mourn, process, accept, apologize, forgive, and do what needs to be done. Just don't delay yourself by dwelling. The joy of the Lord is your strength (Nehemiah 8:10), and He wants to fill and fuel you out of the abundance of His love to keep pressing forward. Yes, we need to own up to our past, but our past doesn't own us any longer. Christ does.

I encourage you to take all the time you need with the Lord, with a counselor or mentor, and with your Christian community to process areas of your life you need to revisit and work through. I had to do all those things, and I am especially thankful for my amazing husband, Richard, for being a consistent source of truth that calls out the shame I sometimes view myself through. He has sat with me, listened to me, encouraged me, and remained kind and faithful to speak the truth in love over me, and even rebuke the unkind ways I sometimes judge myself for my mistakes. He has shown me the gentleness of God in so many ways and how to be gracious toward myself when needed. Pausing to process is healthy, normal, and necessary to keep moving forward. Acknowledging the past hurt and decisions is part of healing. But once that has been dealt with, start running the race without the burden of what God has forgiven and freed you from!

Don't Bring It with You

We all have comfort shows that remind us of our childhood. I was completely obsessed with *The Brady Bunch*. I watched old reruns with my mom, tried to dress up like Marcia Brady for school, and even asked for the entire DVD set for my birthday one year. My favorite episodes, aside from Marcia getting hit in the face with a football, chronicled their trip to Hawaii. In that three-part special, one of the three sons finds an old tiki idol that carries bad luck. Crazy things keep happening everywhere they go. They finally discover it is all because of that little cursed idol. They go on a journey to return it to its original burial site in a cave and have to escape a madman archeologist who thinks they stole it.[1] I remember being glued to the TV, wishing they had never picked up that idol and brought it along in the first place.

SOME THINGS ARE BEST LEFT BEHIND BECAUSE THEY'LL ONLY BRING YOU MORE TROUBLE THE LONGER YOU HOLD ON TO THEM.

Some things are best left behind because they'll only bring you more trouble the longer you hold on to them. Maybe it's not a literal Hawaiian tiki idol like the Bradys, but maybe you identify yourself by your worst moments. Maybe it's a toxic community, person, or environment. Maybe it's an activity or hobby that has become an idol in your life. It's hard to part from things that once felt central to your identity or that served as a source of stability, as a crutch, to help carry you through the hard days. But friend, if it's not from God—if it is hindering you more than healing you, pulling you back rather than releasing you into God's purpose for your life—then it may be time to cut the cord.

Transition can be scary, especially if it requires stepping into a place of uncertainty, a lack of control, and a posture of complete abandonment and trust. Whatever your argument for delaying might be, I encourage you *not* to delay. Obey. If God doesn't want you bringing something into the places where He is calling you, just rip off the Band-Aid and do it now. Release and surrender today. He will give you the words and the wisdom to do so, and He will be sure to follow up with His peace and presence to comfort you.

BATTLE PLAN STEP #8:
Let Go and Look Ahead

As we move forward from our past, we must be willing to address issues, heal from them, and release whatever is needed, then move into freedom and forgiveness. Let's not forget these things as we step into God's future for us:

- We have all made mistakes we aren't proud of and gone through circumstances we wish we hadn't. Today, with the ability to look back on those times with new wisdom, maturity, and understanding for sin, we need to extend grace to our past selves who were foolish, didn't know better, and were naive to unfortunate situations they couldn't escape. God extends grace and forgiveness to us, and we need to do that for ourselves.

- We need to be willing to release ourselves from mistakes just like God does. If we dwell on the past and allow it to define us today, we will get stuck in bitterness, resentment, anger, self-hatred, and hopelessness. God gives us freedom and forgiveness through Christ so we can have gratitude, grace, love, acceptance, and understanding for our past selves and live as new creations. Our past doesn't define us any longer; Christ does!

- We need to approach God with our regrets, shame, mistakes, and self-judgment over our old reputations. When we present these things to Him and release what He convicts and calls us to release, He will begin to fill us with godly desires, fresh guidance, and a new identity.

- We also need to release the judgment we have for others—those who evoked shame in us, led us into sin, hurt us because of their own brokenness, and didn't treat us in a Christlike manner. They are sinners just like us, and with the Lord (or even a professional), we can learn how to release them from their debts so we all can live totally free.

CHAPTER TEN

WHY "JUST DO BETTER" DOESN'T WORK

When I say that I practically grew up in a counselor's office, I literally mean that. Whether processing childhood and family trauma, fear and anxiety, relationship problems, my struggle with mental health and self-harming thoughts, or even shame from my sins, I have learned many lessons from trusted counselors over time. I think the two who impacted me most were my counselor at DBU and the one I met with throughout 2022 and still to this day as I write this. Their professional help gifted me healing, as well as a safe space to let my walls down, bring my sin and pain into the light, process and grieve seasons I am not proud of, and actually do the work of healing. If you are considering counseling for anything, including processing your sin and shame, I encourage you to go for it. *Especially* if it is biblically-based counseling.

As much as we need the science and methodology that healing requires, the Word of God and its truth are fundamental to our growth journey as believers.

I remember learning about the science behind our behavior and how repetitions and patterns form within us. When I say this blew my mind, I mean it, because for the first time, I understood *why* I fall back into my sinful ways. It explained why a "just do better" approach wasn't working for me. Perhaps you've heard these words from the apostle Paul and thought, *Yep! That's me all right.* I'm referring to Romans 7:15: "I don't really understand myself, for I want to do what is right, but I don't do it. Instead, I do what I hate" (NLT). I *hate* that I do what I hate. Can you relate? But *why* do you do it? The answer is simple: *because it is what you have always done.*

The Science Behind the Struggle

Here is the thing. I am not a scientific genius. I know, it's hard to believe I'm not Jimmy Neutron or Isaac Newton. In school, my strong suit was always English, not science, so bear with me as I try to simplify the neurobiology of habit formation.

Sure, sin is fun at first. It gives us that fix of dopamine as we satisfy our basic needs. That, combined with a lack of conviction or awareness of truth, causes us to return to our sin to get that dopamine fix again. This association influences repetitive behavior, which then becomes habit. It slowly snowballs into an avalanche we can no longer control. It's automatic, in fact. Whenever we repeat an action, it gets ingrained in our brains through this thing called a *neural pathway.*

One of my counselors explained all this to me by comparing it to a walk through a tall wheat field. Imagine you are in that field, and every day you walk through it the same way. Back and forth, you walk along that trail from point A to point B. Eventually, the wheat you're trampling every day settles into a clear trail. The stalks fall down to make a clean and clear path—like a neural pathway. Following this path becomes automatic as you travel across the field to your destination. You don't think about walking through the high wheat stalks; you take the path that's already established.

Neurons and dendrites make up these neural paths. Neurons send information throughout your brain and nervous system; they are the *messengers*. Dendrites occupy neurons as the cells that receive communication from neurons. They look like little branches and help with memory formation. In habit forming, they are key components because the more you perform an action, the more these dendrites form.[1]

As our brain cells communicate more frequently through these repeated actions, they grow stronger and become more prevalent. The messages travel faster and more frequently. The frequency and speed take us from occasional actions to *automatic compulsions*. They become our new normal, second nature, habitual. Alongside the neurons and dendrites, a significant chemical, dopamine, comes into play. I listened to the podcast *Breakthroughs* featuring Dr. Talia Lerner, assistant professor of neuroscience at Northwestern Medicine's Feinberg School of Medicine. She gave *habit* a specific definition that stuck out to me: "Habits are generally defined as being behaviors that are resistant to change."[2]

She then went on to discuss dopamine as a neuron that doesn't only indicate we are happy. Different types of dopamine neurons influence us to react positively or negatively, assist with predictability, and cultivate habit formation. She specified that dopamine is key to forming habits in specific regions of our brain. (In case you care to know the nitty-gritty details, it's the dorsolateral striatum, where habit forming and learning take place within us.) Lerner's team also focused on the putamen, the center for learning and motor control linked to reward and addiction. She and her team did extensive research on this area of the brain and wanted to know why certain things become habit and others do not. They drew a few conclusions from their study:

1. Dopamine circuits connect stratal subregions, meaning our brains send signals to places like our motor cortex to form addictive patterns and habits. We chemically develop desires to keep these habits—both the destructive ones and the beneficial ones—to experience more dopamine in those regions. If I were to go to the gym every day for the next three months, the dopamine created from moving my body and working out consistently would probably form a habit in me unknowingly, driven by dopamine. That's the only reason I can justify why someone in their right mind would enjoy running a marathon, because my knees ache just thinking about that. It's the dopamine that keeps us motivated! Negatively speaking, it can be hard for people to stop having premarital sex and one-night stands not just because of the emotional intimacy, but also because of the dopamine rush they experience. They keep up that habit because their brain has been trained to seek out that next hit

of dopamine from that associated activity. Lerner's team labeled this finding the *ascending spiral hypothesis* because it involves the progress of an action becoming a goal, then a goal developing into a habit.

2. Similarly, Lerner and her team have unpacked the *descending spiral*, the circuit that allows you to turn a habit back into a goal, and break it down to a simple behavior—a reversal of sorts. They are still conducting ample research on this since it is still in its infancy, but the discovery and possibility alone spur us on to hope that by our will and God's strength we can experience freedom and change in our habits and desires even at the molecular level. Things don't have to stay the same! You don't have to keep getting distracted, derailed, and discouraged by desires that destroy you. Change, transformation, and freedom are not just promises of God but intricately knit within us by Him, even down to the smallest detail of how our brain and body cooperate with His will and order for things.

YOU DON'T HAVE TO KEEP GETTING DISTRACTED, DERAILED, AND DISCOURAGED BY DESIRES THAT DESTROY YOU.

I know this is a whole lot of science babble, but I really believe it is important to note. We need to break down the struggle with sin so we can break away from it. It's not just "in your head" but literally in your head. Research confirms and explains what the Bible says. How cool and affirming is that? Knowing all this information—the 101 of neurobiology for dopamine and habit forming—it makes sense that the more you walk out the path you've paved, the more distinct the path can get. But here's the thing: even with hopes of descending spiral research still to come, we can't just try to dig up the wheat stalks we've walked all over and make them stand perfectly straight again. We have already made a distinct path in our brains and in our actions. That is where many of us get it wrong. We try to go back and fix the neuropathways we have made by our own will and might. If we can't backtrack and reverse the neuropathway ourselves as far as we know now, what

> WE HAVE TO FORM *NEW* PATHS, INGRAIN *NEW* HABITS, AND START MAKING *THOSE* HEALTHY REPETITIVE BEHAVIORS AND THOUGHTS IN OUR LIVES.

can we actually and practically do? Simple. We have to form *new* paths, ingrain *new* habits, and start making *those* healthy repetitive behaviors and thoughts in our lives.

Science and the Scriptures

I think the concepts Lerner revealed in her research complement what Paul detailed in Romans 7:15—that at a spiritual and neurobiological level, we keep doing what we don't want to do, even though our hearts and souls have been saved and redeemed by Jesus. In Lerner's definition, habits are not just what we do repetitively, but they are *resistant* and *reluctant* to change, even though deep down in our hearts, we *want* to stop.

This may sound like dooming news.

Really, Kirby?

My sinful, habitual compulsions are resistant and reluctant to change?

Is there any hope for me after all?

Yes! There is tremendous hope for you! The good news is, although the paved path may not be completely irreversible in our own strength, God is paving a *new* path in you. By the power of His Holy Spirit in you, you can be free! You can choose His new path for your life and walk it out. You can formulate new habits and cultivate new desires. He will also graciously and generously give you new desires and the strength to pursue them instead of your old ways. Jesus is with you every step of the way to guide, protect, and reveal to you His perfect plans for your life. Like we talked about earlier, sanctification is the process of being perfected and purified daily to look more like Christ. It is a *process*—something I cannot emphasize enough—that takes place from the moment we profess faith in Christ and submit to His lordship until we are in heaven with Him. We are going on a *journey* of freedom. We are fully free, but it takes time for us to unlearn our old way of living and to learn the new steps, patterns, and ways of living out the freedom God has given us. As Romans 6:22 says, "But now that you have been set free from sin and have become slaves of God, the fruit you get leads to sanctification and its end, eternal life" (ESV). Life, friend, is on the other side of this journey of freedom and sanctification!

ALTHOUGH THE PAVED PATH MAY NOT BE COMPLETELY IRREVERSIBLE IN OUR OWN STRENGTH, GOD IS PAVING A *NEW* PATH IN YOU.

Hear me loud and clear: I do believe God can heal us of our addictions in an instant. I am 100% convinced that Jesus can change the heart, behaviors, actions, and molecular structure of our neurobiology in a moment. He is a miracle worker. He is God.

He is Lord of all. He is the Author and Creator of life who knit you in your mother's womb (Psalm 139:13). But the other side to that reality is that sometimes God doesn't do things in an instant. Oftentimes, we go through sanctification over time to realize our sins, turn away from them, and choose to love and follow God. We mature as we are made new daily. I'm sure many of us would prefer instant change, myself included. I very much wish that God would make everything that is wrong with me right in the snap of a finger. Every illness, inclination, and insecurity. But God has His reasonings, plans, and purposes in gifting us this process of growth, because it ultimately grows us (through our free will) closer to Him.

It's not always easy, it's not always fun, and it's oftentimes not short. Think of sanctification as a big family road trip with plenty of highways, stop signs, traffic lights, and sightseeing. God will give us directions to get us going, but He is the One who maps out our course. It is a beautiful journey led by the hand of God, with His mercy all over it. His timing is all through-out it. He knows how we feel, what we think, what we do, and what we have done, and He helps us take the proper steps to be made new. He doesn't force a standard of perfection on us overnight, and I am so thankful for that, because one, it's impossible, and two, I would be crushed under that weight of performance. God is not seeking a performance from you but proximity with you. He wants to be near to you, to do life with you, and to redeem you daily through the perfecting process of sanctification. He wants to help you walk new paths, live a new life, and have a renewed way of seeing the world.

GOD IS NOT SEEKING A PERFORMANCE FROM YOU BUT PROXIMITY WITH YOU.

Renewing Our Minds

When I became at Christian at the age of fourteen, I wanted to know the Bible. Sure, I had seen a few *VeggieTales* episodes here and there and would say my bedtime prayers growing up, but I didn't really know God. I wanted to know Him like Moses knew Him—as a friend (Exodus 33:11). I wanted to know His heart, His ways, His voice, and I wanted to know how to live my life drawing nearer to Him. I knew very little about the Bible at the beginning of my faith journey, but I knew that Scripture was the foundation on which I could build my faith and know the one true God.

I remember going to a Christian bookstore and buying a book on Romans 12. The back cover said it would help Christians build their faith and grow in their calling as a Christ follower. *Perfect*, I thought. I purchased it, read it cover to cover, and really began to understand how to read Scripture, interpret the Bible, ask questions, and apply it in my life. After that deep study, Romans 12 became one of my all-time favorite Scripture passages—particularly verse 2:

> Do not conform to the pattern of this world, but be transformed by the renewing of your mind. Then you will be able to test and approve what God's will is—his good, pleasing and perfect will.

As Christians, we go through a process in which our minds are conformed to a new way of functioning, thinking, and living. That is the only way we can let go of our past self and embrace all God has for us as new creations. If we are to embrace this new life of freedom and see our past sins and struggles fall away, renewing our mind is essential, and this happens as we store up His truth in our minds, meditate on it, and memorize it.

This daily process counteracts the habits and sin cycles we've typically operated in, and it centers on the truth of God's Word. When we fill our minds with truth about our sin, real life, God's character, the Enemy's nature, and who we're called and created to be, that renewed mind leads to a renewed heart, then renewed conduct, and from there a renewed life. We find freedom from our old ways. It's not just a matter of "doing better" and "trying harder"; it's an organic overflow of truth that sets us free (John 8:31–32). Let's break this down, because this is a major key to unlocking freedom in your life.

God's Truth Sets You Free

The ball is in your court regarding the transformative process of renewing your mind. You choose whether to put in the work on the court to shoot those three-pointers. Romans 12:2 encourages believers to conform their minds, will, and ways to those of Christ. Here is the thing, though: you and I can only know how Christ lived, thought, and taught by getting into God's Word. Renewing your mind involves wiping the dust off your Bible, cracking open its spine, and taking in all its truth.

Second Timothy 3:16–17 tells us, "All Scripture is God-breathed and is useful for teaching, rebuking, correcting

> **RENEWING YOUR MIND INVOLVES WIPING THE DUST OFF YOUR BIBLE, CRACKING OPEN ITS SPINE, AND TAKING IN ALL ITS TRUTH.**

and training in righteousness, so that the servant of God may be thoroughly equipped for every good work." I feel like our world shrugs off the Bible as some outdated rule book, but it has more than just wise commands that guide us and guard us. It is God's self-revelation. The beauty of the Bible is that when you read it, it also reads you. There is something unique and miraculous that happens when we dive into those pages, seeking to know God's heart and hear His voice. He still speaks to us today through His Word, and that renews us from the clutter and chatter of wickedness, lies, and sin that try to conform our mind to a counterfeit way of living. The simple truth? You simply need the truth! Because when you taste and see its goodness and honesty, you won't want to return to the fake fixes this world has to offer that your flesh foolishly falls for.

Romans 10:17 says, "Consequently, faith comes from hearing the message, and the message is heard through the word about Christ." To renew our minds, we need to *hear* God's Word. I love church for many reasons, community and worship included. However, my favorite part of Sunday service is hearing my pastor read the Word of God and preach it. We need to hear it spoken in our lives, whether someone reads it out loud to us or we do this in our daily devotions with God. Sometimes instead of listening to music or podcasts in the car, I'll just listen to audio readings of the Bible, because I know my soul needs it. On those days when I feel weak, after those moments I've behaved out of character, it has grounded me to remember who I am, whose I am, and how I now can live my life as a beloved and freed child of God. If you've never done that, I encourage you to give it a try. Hearing God's Word shapes our minds daily for the better, building up our faith in Him. I know on days when I am filled with it, everything changes for the better, even if it is a hard day.

Not Only Hearers, but Readers!

On top of hearing the Word of God, we need to read it. It's one thing to listen to a pastor, podcast, or audio recording of the Bible, but it's a whole other thing to spend quality time soaking it all in for yourself. We need to set aside time in our day, every day, to read God's Word and study it. We do this to meet with God, hear His voice, and know more about Him, ourselves, and the world around us, but we also read it to apply its principles and instruction to our lives. When I was in high school, I made God's Word a priority because I wanted to know Him more. I wanted guidance to love others better, have a more fulfilling life, and overcome my sin. In between honors classes, drama club, cheerleading, my social life, and church volunteering, I still made time for God in my day. Sometimes all I could realistically give God was five minutes. Other days it was thirty. I gave Him whatever I could offer, and He blessed that time I committed to Him. It wasn't just about the minutes spent, but the intention and heart behind it that God loved, desired, and honored. It was about the quality of that time spent with God, not just the quantity.

At first it felt a little awkward, like sitting at the table with the new kid, trying to find connection points so we could get to know each other better. I didn't know what to read, what some of the stories and Christian phrases meant, or how my pastor was able to preach so much about it. So I wrote down my questions, asked God for clarity and answers, and kept on reading, researching, and reaching out to my pastor to help me understand all the Lord had put in this book for me to know. I didn't learn the entire Bible overnight. Even now, with a masters in theology and more than a decade after my salvation, I still don't know every single detail about the Bible and the history and culture behind it. But I do know more today than I did then, because I have spent time in God's Word!

Can You Call His Truth to Mind?

Have you ever met a person who can quote Scripture out of nowhere? Like, they have a verse for every occasion? That's not only impressive but important, because in moments of temptation, trial, decision-making, and the testing of our will and character, we need to be able to remember the truth. When you are in bed alone at night and feel tempted to re-download that app you know is toxic, you need to be able to whip out Galatians 2:20 to fight off the attack of the Enemy. When you're in a heated debate with your spouse and feel like landing a low blow with angry words, you need to recall 1 Corinthians 1:10 so you can resist your flesh damaging that relationship. When you've vowed to quit the online shopping addiction but get a text that your favorite store is having a cyber sale, you need to be able to call to mind James 1:12 and stand firm in your conviction to honor God in the areas where you're susceptible.

MEMORIZING SCRIPTURE ISN'T JUST ABOUT QUOTING IT TO QUOTE IT BUT TO BE ABLE TO CALL IT TO MIND WHEN THE WAR BEGINS.

There are so many verses that not only encourage us but *empower us* to hold firm in obedience to God and refuse compromise. We need to hear God's Word, read God's Word, and memorize it. Memorizing Scripture isn't just about quoting it to quote it but to be able to call it to mind when the war begins.

War? Kirby, I did not join JROTC. I am not Maverick from Top Gun. I am no G.I. Joe, Avenger, or Forrest Gump. What do you mean war? Surprise! We are in a very real war against the Enemy, and Ephesians 6 clearly states this. Verse 12 specifies our enemy: "For we do not wrestle against flesh and blood, but against principalities, against powers, against the rulers of the darkness of this age, against spiritual hosts of wickedness in the heavenly places" (NKJV). We are fighting a spiritual war—a literal one. It's serious, and the Enemy is doing all he can to take ground in our lives. He will lure us away to ambush us. He will drop atomic bombs when we least expect it. He will fire flaming darts from afar so we'll run and take cover. But no need to fear; the Lord fights for us (Deuteronomy 3:22; Isaiah 54:17; Psalm 34:17; Romans 8:31) and equips us as a soldier for battle with the sword of the Spirit, aka *the Word of God* (Ephesians 6:17). Second Corinthians 10:3–5 sums up our weaponry and strategy best: "For though we live in the world, we do not wage war as the world does. The weapons we fight with are not the weapons of the world. On the contrary, they have divine power to demolish strongholds. We demolish arguments and every pretension that sets itself up against the knowledge of God, and we take captive every thought to make it obedient to Christ." We need to memorize the Word because it helps us understand God's voice, giving us new vocabulary to communicate clearly with Him. It also serves as weaponry against the lies, schemes, and flaming arrows of the Enemy (Ephesians 6:16). It keeps us sharp so we can be prepared at any moment for any attack.

Chew the Cud

Along with hearing, reading, and memorizing God's Word, we also need to meditate on it. I'm not talking about sitting crisscross-applesauce, hands on knees, chanting, "Ommmmm." I'm also not talking about the Eastern forms of meditation linked to different religions or spiritual connections. The biblical term for meditating means "to chew the cud." It references how cows eat and digest their food, which initially enters their first stomach (yeah, their first). They then regurgitate that food and it returns to their mouth as cud to be chewed a second time. And it doesn't stop there. A cow has four stomachs—you do the math on how much cud a cow chews.

In the same way, we are to meditate on the Word of God. Rather than reading a few chapters at a time during your daily devotions, I encourage you to take time to really chew on the verses you read, digest them, and revisit them over and over again. Ask questions; mull them over; really digest what God is saying. Get all the nutrients and information out. In Joshua 1:8, God instructs His people, saying, "This Book of the Law shall not depart from your mouth, but you shall meditate on it day and night, so that you may be careful to do according to all that is written in it. For then you will make your way prosperous, and then you will have good success" (ESV). Psalm 119:97 says, "How I love your instruction! Every day it is my meditation" (ISV).

A renewed mind is developed by hearing, reading, studying,

memorizing, and meditating on the Word of God. Freedom comes from truth, and the Bible is God's revelation, explanation, and historic record of truth. As you get to know God personally and spend time in His Word, you will be freed to fight against the lies of the Enemy and see through the temptations of this world.

Having the Mind of Christ

Paul wrote in 1 Corinthians 2:16, "'Who has understood the mind of the Lord so as to instruct him?' But we have the mind of Christ" (ESV). This verse is not saying we have the same amount of knowledge, status, wisdom, or authority as God. Neither is it making the audacious claim that we *are* Christ or a type of Christ as some distorted New Age beliefs claim. When Paul mentioned the mind of Christ, he meant that through Christ, we get to share in the knowledge of His *perspective*, plans, and purposes for our lives.

THROUGH CHRIST, WE GET TO SHARE IN THE KNOWLEDGE OF HIS *PERSPECTIVE*, PLANS, AND PURPOSES FOR OUR LIVES.

Back in 2021, Ryan Reynolds starred in a movie called *Free Guy*, which is pretty fitting for this book, huh? In it, one of the non-player characters (NPCs) within a video game world becomes sentient and discovers he is actually a video game character, not a real person, thanks to the help of a real person playing the video game. The female game player gives him glasses so he can view the online world for what it really is, showcasing the actual elements of the game he otherwise could not have seen. This is what I think having the mind of Christ is like—putting on a special pair of glasses that helps you see things as they truly are.

Scripture is the lens by which we can see the world correctly, the order in which God created things, and how they are meant to be. When we live within that order, you and I get to experience peace, joy, and an abundant life firsthand. When we live outside of it, we experience the effects of disorder. The pain, hurt, suffering, and sin we endure today were never meant to be part of our everyday life, but because of sin and a broken world full of sinful people, we walk through these difficulties. But thank the Lord we don't have to go through it alone! We have Jesus. He can redeem anything you've ever gone through, are going through, or will go through into something beautiful that can testify of His goodness.

Sadly, without a biblical worldview, it's easy for people to have a distorted view of God and His Word. They aren't wearing the *Free Guy* glasses. The world often looks at the Bible, the guidance and commands God gives us, as foolish. They don't have the ability to see it for what it is. As believers, however, we can see the goodness of God and His Word and their value to our life.

God doesn't tell us to do or not do things just to mess with us or to run some cynical social experiment. He has our best interest in mind. He really, truly cares about us, our hearts, our desires, our concerns, and everything in between. If what He says about Himself is true (which it is)—that He is good, kind, forgiving, gracious, just, merciful, loving, and true—shouldn't we trust in His plans for us? The Holy Spirit gives us the mind of Christ and matures us to understand the world and our wicked ways in light of Christ's glory and grace (1 Corinthians 2:14–16). This knowledge, although sobering and mournful at times, grows us in gratitude and produces a celebratory spirit of thanksgiving and freedom within us. The mind of Christ gives us vision, humbles us to see our sin for what it is, helps us to say yes to God's way of life, and empowers us to abandon sin for the good gifts He has for us instead.

The Eighteen-Inch Journey

We need a renewed mind and *heart* to live a renewed life. In Proverbs 4:23, we find these very wise words: "Above all else, guard your heart, for everything you do flows from it." Knowledge, belief, information, assumptions, and our perception of reality flow through our mind. We can acknowledge something as true, but God wants His truth to take root in our lives as conviction, a deeply personal and intimate knowing. That is where the heart comes into play. It is personal. It is linked with the will and emotion center and is central to our intentions, which influence our decisions. I could very well know that eating junk food for breakfast, lunch, and dinner every day is bad for me, but my convictions could be so weak that my actions still lead me to do whatever I want. Trust me, I once ate s'mores for breakfast for an entire week, and that stomachache was enough to show me I had made a very bad judgment call.

There are horrible consequences to living with destructive habits, whether physical, mental, emotional, or spiritual. I am talking more than s'mores now, alright?

> WE CAN ACKNOWLEDGE SOMETHING AS TRUE, BUT GOD WANTS HIS TRUTH TO TAKE ROOT IN OUR LIVES AS CONVICTION, A DEEPLY PERSONAL AND INTIMATE KNOWING.

Our *minds* need to be filled with the knowledge and fear of the Lord, but that is not enough. It must travel down eighteen inches and become a convicting reality within our hearts, causing our will and the way we live to bow to Jesus' lordship. God wants you to know Him not only intellectually but *intimately* as well. Intimacy is intentional, personal, deep, and consistent. Jesus declares that loving God is the greatest commandment alongside loving others: "And you shall love the Lord your God with all your heart and with all your soul and with all your mind and with all your strength" (Mark 12:30 ESV). As we went over before, our

GOD WANTS YOU TO KNOW HIM NOT ONLY INTELLECTUALLY BUT *INTIMATELY* AS WELL.

mind, the center for intellect and reasoning; our *soul*, the center for our state of living and personal being; our *strength*, our center for passion and might; and our *heart*, the center of intentions and emotions, should be directed toward God. Our direction reveals our affection. Our devotion reveals what we cherish most. If we are pursuing an intimate and intentional relationship with the Lord and loving Him and His truth with our everything, our desires and affections will experience redemption.

Doing Away with Destructive Desires

Loving God with every part of us helps us break sinful habits and develop righteous ways of living. Growing in friendship with God and understanding His purposes redeems our desires and develops new ones within us. They play a huge part in freedom from habitual sin. Remember the wheat field analogy from earlier? As much as we need to deny the flesh, we need to *cultivate* new desires and begin treading a new path, the narrow path Christ calls us to walk (Matthew 7:13–14). We should not only spend our attention, time, and effort leaving behind old, destructive tendencies. We need to direct *more energy* toward cultivating godly desires, biblical inclinations, and holy habits—not focusing on the positive and ignoring the negative, but feeding the spirit and starving the flesh.

> LOVING GOD WITH EVERY PART OF US HELPS US BREAK SINFUL HABITS AND DEVELOP RIGHTEOUS WAYS OF LIVING.

As I mentioned earlier, I went to Sky Ranch Christian Camp every summer for ten years as a camper and even worked there after I graduated high school as a camp counselor for two years. This was the place where I learned about Jesus and eventually got saved. The summer I turned fifteen, my camp small group and I began sharing in Bible study how defeated we felt by our ongoing struggles with sin. How come we felt so secure and strong in our convictions at camp, then a few weeks after going home, slipped back into the same old ways? That's when our counselor began to tell us about dogfights.

Who Are You Feeding?

I was not expecting her to use a dogfight as an analogy for sin. She asked us, "If two dogs are in a dogfight, which one will win?" We were all a bit startled and looked around in confusion. We asked about the dog breeds, size differences, and demeanors. She interrupted us and said, "The dog that will win is the one you feed." I know that's a gruesome example, and I for one am very opposed to dogfights and animal abuse, but that graphic picture has always stuck with me. *Whichever dog gets fed will win.* If the other is starving, it won't put up a winning fight.

This is the battle between the Spirit and the flesh within us. The Spirit desires to do what is good, right, pure, and admirable (Philippians 4:8). The flesh desires to satisfy its instant needs by whatever means necessary, ignoring the boundaries and order God has established to protect us, provide for us, and cultivate peace within us. When we are faced with a choice, either our spirit or our flesh influences us, and the one we feed more has greater power to persuade us. Here's the good news: we can change who we give that authority to. If your fleshly desires puppeteer you into making decisions that destroy you, you can cut off their supply and start feeding your spirit instead.

IT'S OFTEN THE LITTLE THINGS WE BRUSH OFF THAT LEAD US TO BIG COMPROMISES DOWN THE ROAD.

By spending time in God's Word, worship, godly community, prayer, fasting, and eliminating worldly influences, the Spirit has room to grow and shape your life for the better. Personally, I had to cut out watching certain TV shows because they influenced me to think, speak, and act out of character and in opposition to who God created me to be. It was hard to let go of those shows and cut out that entertainment, but at the end of the day, they were leading me to entertain what compromised my character, and that wasn't worth it.

I know that's a small example, but media, music, hobbies, environments, social gatherings, and possessions may need to take a back seat in your life to make room for the Holy Spirit to help you get your life on track. It's often the little things we brush off that lead us to big compromises down the road. If you feel that inkling to remove something from your life to give God more influence, *do it*. Rip off the Band-Aid now, because the quicker you obey those convictions, the quicker you'll get to enjoy peace and freedom and gain clarity for God's will.

JUST BECAUSE MY SINFUL DESIRES WON A BATTLE DOESN'T MEAN THE ENEMY WON THE WAR.

Our life is composed of a series of battles that make up one large war—against the flesh, the Enemy, and the wicked ways of this world. I know some of us have suffered defeat in the past, but you do not have to live there any longer. I've had my fair share of battle scars from victories and failures, but just because my sinful desires won a battle doesn't mean the Enemy won the war. Last time I checked, Christ has already won, and we get to partake in that same victory. Jesus said in John 16:33, "I have said these things to you, that in me you may have peace. In the world you will have tribulation. But take heart; I have overcome the world" (ESV). First Corinthians 15:57 echoes this, saying, "But thanks be to God, who gives us the victory through our Lord Jesus Christ" (ESV). We fight from a place of victory! Allow yourself to embrace this with confidence: you are fighting a battle in a war already won.

BATTLE PLAN STEP #9:
Make Over Your Mind

With a renewed mind, the mind of Christ, and an understanding of how God created our brains in the first place, let us go on to do good, to choose our actions wisely, and to let our affections and directions line up with God's way. Remember these truths and let them take root in your mind and heart today:

- Our struggle against sin is not only spiritual but scientific. God designed us and knows exactly how our brains work with habits, addictions, and patterns. That is another reason He calls us to obedience. He knows how hard we can struggle to break free from sin, even at the basic molecular level. However, we still have hope and proof that we can retrain our brains, renew our minds, and develop the mind of Christ with God's help.

- Our first step in renewal includes renewing our minds with truth. By hearing, reading, studying, memorizing, and meditating on God's Word, its truth will free us. Lies will begin to unravel, convictions will calcify, and confidence to resist and overcome the Enemy and his schemes will become easier for us, because truth empowers us and sets us free.

- Our hearts also need renewal. Knowing and believing truth wholeheartedly completes our battle strategy. You can know Christ has the power to save, but unless you believe it's true for you, too, you will never experience total victory. Freedom requires faith.

- Our desires will shift and change as God renews our hearts and minds by His truth. We will no longer lust over lies, chase after counterfeits, or surrender to schemes, knowing the folly behind it all. We might not be able to backtrack and get those old wheat stalks to stand, but it's never too late to start walking a new, narrow, redeemed path. God can cultivate new desires within you today.

CHAPTER ELEVEN

FROM DISCIPLINE TO DESIRE

I am not Katniss Everdeen by any means, but I do know one thing about archery—it's where we get our word *sin* from. To *sin* literally means to miss the mark. In the game of archery and the game of life, I am 100% a sinner. I have missed the mark more times than I've hit a bullseye. But I know that if I dedicated my time, efforts, and intellect toward learning how to shoot a bow and arrow properly, that discipline would shape how I shoot. My aim would improve. I would know how to adjust my form and shoot my arrow given the direction of the wind or the distance of my target. Disney's archery expert, Princess Merida, may have been onto something when she asked, "If you had the chance to change your fate, would ya?" Let me ask you this: If you had the chance to change your desires, would ya?

Maybe that feels like an impossible task and a far-fetched ask, but honestly, if you could, would you? I guarantee that answer is yes. Our desires are revealed through our actions, so if we want to change what we do, we have to change our desires. The remedy isn't to shove them down and suppress them or to gaslight yourself and pretend they aren't there. That will only provide the right conditions

IT'S NOT ABOUT HIDING YOUR HABITUAL SINS BUT SEEING WHAT HEALTHY, GODLY OPTIONS YOU CAN SUBSTITUTE INSTEAD.

for them to fester in your life and slowly intoxicate you from the inside out, until you can't take it anymore. I honestly think that is one of the main reasons why so many people leave the church and feel as though God won't help them get better. It's not about hiding your habitual sins but seeing what healthy, godly options you can substitute instead. Not just removing what you struggle with but finding a holy habit to implement that will give you life and change your trajectory. We want to live fruitful and bountiful lives, not wither and waste away.

Bountiful Blooms and Growing Gardens

All throughout the Bible there are farming and gardening analogies. One analogy often used in the New Testament is planting seeds and bearing fruit. We don't have to be agricultural experts to understand the basics of that example. One major mark of the Christian life is *fruitfulness*. Whatever gets planted in our lives bears fruit. Bad seeds bear bad fruit, and good seeds bear good fruit. Pretty simple.

The fruit of the Spirit is a key example of this. Galatians 5:22–23 lists these as evidence that the Spirit of God is within the life of a believer: love, joy, peace, patience, kindness, goodness, faithfulness, gentleness, and self-control. He is the One who plants that seed in us and helps us, nurtures us, grafts us, prunes us, and grows us to see it bloom in our day-to-day decisions and interactions. But to bear fruit and partake in the beautiful, bountiful blooms, we have to yield to God's pruning process and submit to what He wants sown in our lives.

Pruning requires unnecessary branches to be cut off. Why? Because they take away nutrients (life) from other branches that need it. Don't be surprised as you read this book if God highlights an area of your life that is life-sucking, not life-giving, that He wants to prune so you can live healthier than you previously did.

GOOD THINGS, AND GOD THINGS, OFTEN TAKE TIME AND TRUST.

It hurts to have vines, branches, and twigs snipped, but the fruitfulness that comes from that gesture leads to far better and godlier growth.

This process takes trust and time, two things that define discipline very well.

Disciplines aren't always fun initially, and I believe that's because we want instant results. But good things, and God things, often take time and trust. The bountiful blooms to come will prove that.

Let's discuss what realignment with God looks like. It requires discipline, and although it can be challenging and test our patience at times, the new fruit and desires that truly glorify God and are good for us thrive when God prunes the fruit of destructive desires.

Disciplines Develop Desires

I have never been good at keeping New Year's resolutions. By the second week or sometimes the second day, I've already failed to keep my commitments. One year I wanted to take up crocheting and get really good at making my own sweaters and blankets. I couldn't figure out how to make my first stitch and gave up instantly. Another year I got a skateboard and was determined to learn how to do all sorts of kicks and flips. I ate concrete every single time and gave up after I nearly broke my elbow. I still have the board collecting dust in my garage. But in 2023, I decided I wanted to follow through with my resolution, so I chose a fitness challenge called 75 Hard. It is a mental and physical challenge to do the following every day for 75 days straight, no exceptions: work out for 45 minutes indoors, work out for another 45 minutes outdoors, read 10 pages of a book, drink a gallon of water, stick to a diet of your choice, cut out alcohol, and take a progress picture every. single. day. The catch? If you fail in any of these, you have to start over from day 1 the following day. I was determined to succeed. Guess what happened next?

On day 12 I failed. For almost two weeks, I stuck to everything on that list and was doing so well, until I faced a moment of temptation with my diet and decided to make an exception. In the moment, it felt great to satisfy my craving, but when I got into bed that night to check off my accomplishments for the day's regimen, the conviction hit. I'd gone against the rules. I had to start over the next day. I was so upset with myself, because after eleven successful days, I caved into my desires rather than sticking to the disciplines I was forming. I might have failed, but I didn't stay defeated. I decided to stay disciplined and see it through. I wanted to overcome the challenge and tell others I had put my mind, heart, and body into it and accomplished the goal through my discipline. And I did it! I successfully completed 75 Hard!

That initial failure gave me so much perspective on how much it sucks to fail and how much more rewarding it is at the end of the day to stay disciplined, even when temptation calls out. God ended up teaching me a lot through the whole process. I felt Him impress upon me the truth that it's so easy to give up and so much harder to keep going, not just in a workout challenge like this but in any obstacle or challenge we go through, especially in overcoming our habitual sinful desires.

No Quit, No Compromise

During my second-round attempt, temptations still came at me left and right. You don't think I wanted to sneak some Chick-fil-A nuggets into my diet? Or binge-watch Netflix instead of reading at the end of a long day of grad school and work? Don't even get me started on two workouts a day for 75 days straight, even if I had a migraine, under scorching sun or blizzarding snow. I stayed disciplined, committed, and consistent even when my feelings and desires tried to move me otherwise. I don't think emotions are bad. However, we aren't supposed to be led by our ever-changing feelings (Ephesians 4:26; Proverbs 3:5). We are led by truth. I was able to remain disciplined, committed, and consistent because I knew deep down that I would feel good, more accomplished, and more fulfilled doing what I was supposed to, even when I didn't feel like it in that moment. I knew I could do it! I knew it would be worth it! Remembering what it felt like to fall was enough to keep me from crossing that boundary again. At that point, I no longer allowed "What if I just" and "Maybe I could just" in my vocabulary or my head. I knew the consequences of compromise, and I had to be adamant and rooted in my own convictions not to give in or entertain any thoughts that went with them. Knowing the truth and sticking to godly conviction will empower you to resist compromise and the schemes of Satan.

When my 75 Hard ended, so many of those disciplines had become automatic routines and desires in me, and I felt better because of it. I saw physical transformations in my health that I was proud of. I slept better at night and had genuine energy throughout my day. Through my disciplines I developed new desires, because I saw the impact they truly had on my life for the better. Did I feel this way on day 5, or day 12, or day 26? Not really. But by day 75, I felt like a completely new person in the best way, and I wished I had known just how good it would feel to come out the other side victorious that first time I failed.

Change from the Inside Out

The most rewarding result of 75 Hard was not outward but inward change. My discipline for waking up and working out, eating right, and spending more time reading went from "I *have* to do this" to "I *get* to do this" to "I *want* to do this." This can be true for any discipline and any area of our lives. We waste so much time trying to prevent an action when it comes to instilling new disciplines. I know for me, that only magnifies its power in my mind. If I were to tell you to not think of a blue elephant, what would your mind immediately picture? It's hard to focus on not doing something! However, when I find something else to focus on *implementing*, the time and effort spent on learning, doing, and integrating the activity into my life create a new pathway in my head, but also my heart. Many of my bad habits started to fade away as I began magnifying new ways of living, thinking, spending my time and energy, cultivating habits, and believing.

One primary challenge of 75 Hard was getting up early in the morning. Sure, there were some days when I needed to sleep in due to my migraines and health, but as someone who will gladly sleep in until eleven if given the chance, I became more disciplined in waking up early to hit my goals and get more done during my day. I eliminated one bad discipline just by cultivating one good one. Now I actually want to wake up early, because I understand the reward of it. I didn't just get my workout done, but from that one change, I got more work done, ate better food, spent more time with God at the start of my day, and lessened the anxiety of the rush. The domino effect of discipline has remained in my mornings to this day!

Okay, Kirby, I love that you are able to wake up early, but what are some daily disciplines that help us in our training against habitual sin?

I'm so glad you asked!

Seven Daily Disciplines to Get Spiritually Strong

These are the different spiritual disciplines that have helped me grow in my love for God, related to the temptations I battle.

Perhaps by implementing one of these today and sticking with it, you will notice subtle changes that will yield greater transformation. Like an oyster creating a pearl from a single grain of sand, spiritual maturity, development, and growth take *time*, as do all good and valuable things.

LIKE AN OYSTER CREATING A PEARL FROM A SINGLE GRAIN OF SAND, SPIRITUAL MATURITY, DEVELOPMENT, AND GROWTH TAKE *TIME*.

1. Get in the Word

First, develop a routine and relationship with God's Word, the Bible. We've talked about this a lot already, but if we are going to discern lies, temptations, and what is good and true, then we need to consult Scripture, the written record of God's truth. It is a means by which He still communicates to us today. When we crack open the binding of those sixty-six inspired and inerrant books and give Him permission to read and search our hearts as we read and search the pages, transformation and wonders start taking place. Authentic communion, true abiding, and actual time spent in God's Word foster a deep knowing and a deep love for God, along with real recognition of His pursuit after us. Read His Word, study it, meditate on it, memorize it, apply it, and sift deeply through its many truths and teachings, and be transformed. If you make a habit of this, those ungodly habits will begin to lose their appeal and authority over your life.

2. Practice Prayer

Second, sow into your spiritual maturity with prayer. I'm not just talking about praying for our fast food to "nourish our bodies" or a "God bless everyone I know" before you trail off to

PRAYER POSITIONS US TOWARD GOD, POSTURES OUR HEART FOR THE THINGS OF GOD, AND GIVES US PERSPECTIVE ON THE HEART OF GOD.

sleep at night. I see reading Scripture as the time when God most pours into me, and prayer when I most pour out to God. I not only make my requests known to Him and call on Him for provision, strength, guidance, and wisdom; I reflect and thank God for all He has done and who He is in my life. Prayer brings about *thankfulness* within my life that *recognizes* God's hand in it. Prayer positions us toward God, postures our heart for the things of God, and gives us perspective on the heart of God.

Prayer journaling reveals how God has grown and matured me. It's not often we relive those moments of struggle and recognize our headspace in certain decisions and seasons. We can praise God fully for how He has moved since then. It's interesting to flip through my own journal and see how God has changed ungodly desires, and how my prayers shifted toward truly desiring the things of God over the things of this world. Gratitude and thanksgiving have become abundant in my life since I made a habit of journaling. For the sake of praising God and processing your current situation, write down your prayers. It's a beautiful way to see your transformation journey as well as His faithfulness to you.

3. Integrate Fasting

Third, consider the discipline of fasting. This doesn't always constitute not eating. Dieting and fasting are completely different in motive and in result. Dieting involves changing what and how you eat to achieve a physical or health-based outcome. Fasting is all about intentionally seeking the will of God in our lives by removing something we have an appetite for, whether food or something else. For instance, I once fasted from hitting the snooze button for a whole month so I could intentionally give God my mornings. (I had a bad habit of sleeping in and making the excuse I had no time for God in my day.) Another time I fasted from meals for twenty-four hours because I felt convicted to pray and focus on the Lord in that manner. When we fast, our attention shifts toward God from our normal routines.

FASTING GIVES OUR SOUL A CLEANSE, REVEALING WHERE WE RUN IN OUR WANDERING, OUR THOUGHTS, OUR APPETITES, AND OUR DAILY COMFORTS.

Ultimately, fasting encourages and develops a denial of the self and its desires—what we reach for, crave, and find comfort or distraction in. Fasting gives our soul a cleanse, revealing where we run in our wandering, our thoughts, our appetites, and our daily comforts. It gives us a specific opportunity to commune with God and recognize that our core needs are found in and fulfilled by Him. You can fast from food, but also social media, watching movies, the snooze button, gaming, how you spend your time, all sorts of ways! I've always fasted to get my heart right with God and align with His will for me. It also positions our ears to hear and our hearts to be filled by His ministering. We find our supply and satisfaction in Him.

4. Seek Stillness and Solitude

Fourth, stillness and solitude will bring growth in your life and nurture a closer relationship with God. Often, Jesus retreated to be alone with His Father. Community is a beautiful gift from God, something we as believers are encouraged to cultivate. We need each other. I certainly did when I sought freedom from my habitual sin. However, to intentionally grow with God means to meet with Him intimately. When nobody else is around, with all distractions tucked away, among the hustle and bustle of day-to-day life, we need to prioritize sitting in God's presence and simply *being*. We are active for God and accomplish many works as the fruit of our faith, but God is just as pleased and delighted by our stillness and simple abiding with Him; it nurtures our childlike souls to simply sit in the presence of the Father. We need that quality time with Him. We were made for it. We should prioritize our relationship with God as the most important one we have—over our friends, our family, our significant other—over everyone.

WHEN NOBODY ELSE IS AROUND, WITH ALL DISTRACTIONS TUCKED AWAY, AMONG THE HUSTLE AND BUSTLE OF DAY-TO-DAY LIFE, WE NEED TO PRIORITIZE SITTING IN GOD'S PRESENCE AND SIMPLY *BEING*.

If Christ is not central to our life and we detach from time with Him, not only will we suffer from that absence, but our community will get the worst parts of us. The Enemy will also get the worst parts of us and feed into that separation, filling it with fear, shame, doubt, and anything else he can use to keep us from God. Friend, we need intentional time with God, sitting at His feet, *fully present*. Stillness and solitude do not stunt our growth or steal our time. No time is wasted in God's presence. As my friend Aubray once told me, love is spelled T-I-M-E. God wants our undivided, unrushed presence and attention.

5. Exercise Confession

Fifth, I want to highlight confession. We've talked about this a lot already because, believe it or not, it is a discipline. We need to practice it in our lives to grow as followers of Christ. Confession strengthens our fellowship in the community God gives us and creates beautiful unity within the church. Vulnerability and transparency allow healing to begin and invite God's presence in. You already know this was true for me when I shared with those closest to me my struggle with porn. When I confessed, not only did I feel a weight lift off my shoulders; I instantly was met with support and a deeper level of friendship that I truly needed throughout that process of freedom and healing. Confession also strengthens our relationship with God. Bringing our struggles, our mistakes, and our guilt before God leads us into deeper dependence and reliance on Him, as we face our real need for a Savior and meet the unexplainable grace of God.

> **VULNERABILITY AND TRANSPARENCY ALLOW HEALING TO BEGIN AND INVITE GOD'S PRESENCE IN.**

6. Partake in Worship

Sixth, actively instill the discipline of worship in your Christian walk. You don't have to sound like Kari Jobe or Brandon Lake to worship the Lord (although I wish I did). I'll be honest, only the Lord thinks my melodies are a joyful noise. But worship is more than harmonizing, singing lyrics, and putting on a concert for God. Worship requires sacrifice. Worship puts us in a position of trusting everything into the hands of God, surrendering everything at His feet. It's not easy, and at times He asks a lot from us, but the return is far greater than we could ever imagine.

WHEN WE WORSHIP, GOD SHOWS UP.

By living with open hearts and hands, dedicated to serving God and committing everything we do to His glory, we experience peace and joy that is unexplainable; it is a product of His presence. When we worship, God shows up. To be fair, He is always there, but creating a space to glorify Him in our hearts, our families, our workplace, our service, and so on brings about a blessing to our life and the world. Worship acknowledges God and is an act of love toward Him. It is not just something we give, but the way we live our lives set apart for the Lord. We worship God every day as we invite Him in, give Him thanks and praises, and allow our work to reflect His goodness and glory. This discipline is beautiful, because as we pass from this life to the next, we will carry into heaven a heart of worship that loves to love God.

7. Pursue Community

Seventh, I want to touch on gathering with other believers. Gathering and doing life with those who profess Christ strengthens us to run the race at a better pace. I never ran track, but I know that pacing yourself with those around you helps you secure the spot you're after more effectively. We need to run behind those who have gone before us and know the path better, run alongside those who are at the same pace and space in life as us, and run ahead of the next generation who looks up to us and receives our voice in their lives. In high school, I took it upon myself to start a Bible study to bring believers together in my school. In college, I joined a Christian sorority so that I had that intentional community of girls who were running after God. As a married woman, I now plan yearly trips with other women in ministry across the nation so we can rest, pray for one another, and encourage each other in the realms of influence God has placed us in. I also frequently meet with my church's young adult group, make calls with friends, and hang out one-on-one weekly with girls I treasure who know my heart, struggles, and the assignments God has for me.

GATHERING AND DOING LIFE WITH THOSE WHO PROFESS CHRIST STRENGTHENS US TO RUN THE RACE AT A BETTER PACE.

In different seasons within different circles, I've been prayed for, encouraged, challenged, matured, and inspired by the vulnerability, love, and truth shown to me by my fellow brothers and sisters in Christ. I've confessed sins and been ministered to, and have been the one doing the ministering when they've poured out their hearts to me in search of healing and reconciliation with God. None of us are perfect, and we are the first to admit that, but we are chasing after the One who is perfecting us daily, together. This is how we are meant to do life, linking arms and running toward Christ confidently and freely. Being fully surrounded in this way and led by the Spirit of God together makes us an unstoppable force in His kingdom against the Enemy's darkness and demise.

Failing Forward

What happens when we fail, despite all our best efforts and practicing all these disciplines? Friend, hear me when I say there is a big difference between *failing* and being a *failure*. I've often vented in my prayer journal, feeling like a failure when I couldn't break a sin habit. But the truth is, while I failed in my actions, my identity is not rooted in failure. I, Kirby Ann Kelly, am not a failure. My identity is firm as a child of God, and my worth stems from what He thinks about me, not what I have done wrong. In fact, Christ says that in Him, I am a victor. This is clearly communicated in 1 Corinthians 15:57: "But thanks be to God, who gives us the victory through our Lord Jesus Christ" (ESV). This refers to sin and how it no longer rules over us; Christ does. Because of that, we share in His victory on the cross over sin and death. Making a mere mistake and tripping over a temptation doesn't revoke my chances of continuing to run the race well. It doesn't strip me of my salvation. Failure is part of the journey to freedom. It's part of the sanctification process.

FAILURE IS PART OF THE JOURNEY TO FREEDOM.

We don't ditch the journey just because we mess up. We get up right where we are and keep moving forward. God is not an intense sports coach who makes us return to the starting line to run that drill again after we mess up. No, He is a Father who rushes to where we've fallen, helps us up, and keeps walking with us from that point forward. He meets us where we are; He helps us reset our trajectory and pace to move forward on the path He has called us to run on. Is that not the most encouraging thing ever? You don't have to go back to square one and work back to a place of intimacy, right standing, or favor with God. He is with you, right there in that pit you've fallen into. You don't have to waste any time going backward; He'll help you get out and move on.

You have a race to run, and if you fall or fail, *fail forward*. Get back up, dust yourself off, rest in His presence, return to His Word, worship and pray to Him, and get back into that race you were meant to run. He will cover you with grace as you continue to run at a good pace. He wants you to succeed in your journey of overcoming and freedom because He loves you. He is not your angry and frustrated coach; He is your biggest cheerleader! He is going to hype you up and give you what you need to keep on. Whether it's been a week, a month, a year, or a decade, rest assured His grace and mercy are still as ever-present and ever-true for you today. He is willing to help as you take His hand and follow His lead. Remember, He is for you!

YOU HAVE A RACE TO RUN, AND IF YOU FALL OR FAIL, *FAIL FORWARD.*

Consistency vs. Perfection

My husband is such a good man. Because of my chronic migraines, I get loads of neck and head tension. Every night before we go to bed, he gives me the most relieving neck massages to help with the debilitating pain. He could be half asleep when I roll over to ask him to rub my neck, and without question or complaint, he selflessly wakes up to work out the tension so I can get a good night's sleep. Ladies, marry a good, selfless man. And let that go both ways. Be good and selfless to your spouse in the areas where they need your love and support. Knowing how much pain and tension I consistently endure, Richard gifted me with four sessions of muscle tension stretching and massages as a Christmas present in 2022, and I genuinely wept. I knew that for the next month, a stretching assistant, Blair, would provide some extra relief to my neck and shoulders.

I truly believe that God lined up my connection with Blair,

YOU CAN BE FREE

because he not only knew how to stretch my neck and gave me pointers to practice for pain relief at home, but he is a Christian. Blair explained the difference between consistency and perfection as we were talking about fitness goals, and how in all things, we should focus on *consistency over perfection*. If we hold ourselves to the standard of perfection in everything we do, we are bound to fail, destined for disappointment and feeling disqualified. If we approach our goals, our habits, and our healing with perfection as our sole objective, the pressures that surround us will compound and crush us, just as I discussed in the beginning of this book. But if our objective is consistency, to show up and complete the disciplines and devotions we've committed to daily, we will find freedom. The pressure to perform will fall away and make the achievement reasonable, attainable, and actual.

Make consistency your goal, not perfection. It will sustain you over the long haul. It keeps us going. Let's keep moving forward when we blow it, knowing we can learn and grow from it and become who God calls us to be. A bad decision doesn't doom us. A stupid mistake doesn't stunt us. We can stay consistent and see the results of freedom and spiritual maturity. If we hit a bump in the road, it doesn't have to faze us. If we crash and burn, that's okay. We can take a moment to take care of ourselves, adjust, and keep moving in God's direction. Perfectionism will cause you to see yourself as a failure, but consistency will lead you to see yourself as the victor in Christ that you are.

PERFECTIONISM WILL CAUSE YOU TO SEE YOURSELF AS A FAILURE, BUT CONSISTENCY WILL LEAD YOU TO SEE YOURSELF AS THE VICTOR IN CHRIST THAT YOU ARE.

Your disciplines matter. The small ways you implement change through reading the Word, prayer, fasting, stillness, worship, solitude, service, fellowship . . . all those things work together to mature and sanctify you. Spiritual growth is a process and takes some implementing and learning. Stopping your habitual sins is also a process that takes some implementing and learning. Take it one day at a time, and focus on consistency with one godly principle.

Ask the Holy Spirit to guide your focus as you grow closer to Him. Maybe for the next week, you just need to practice consistently reading your Bible. Then make it two weeks. Then three. Once you've got that down, maybe stretch it out a bit longer and start praying and journaling. Then another week. Then another. Perhaps start by cutting social media to only two hours a day. Or replacing social drinking with sparkling water. Or taking a break from bingeing video games after work and spending time with community or family instead. Pick one thing for a time to build up. Building blocks and the long road, friend; that is how we are going to see change. Through consistency, not perfection.

You know why? Because practice makes perfect. Practice also makes permanent. I learned that from my fourth-grade teacher, Ms. Juro. When we get a good rhythm into our lives and a groove for doing the things of God, understanding its value to our life and the kingdom, we will see change that sticks. We don't just

TO BECOME CHRISTLIKE AND THRIVE IN THE PLACES WHERE HE DIRECTS OUR STEPS, WE MUST PACE OURSELVES WITH GRACE, FIND MEANING IN THE MUNDANE, AND DO THE DISCIPLINES THAT WILL DEVELOP RIGHT DESIRES.

want to stop doing what we hate. We want to *start* doing what we deeply desire to do for God. But we all have to start from the basics and not get too far ahead of ourselves. To become Christlike and thrive in the places where He directs our steps, we must pace ourselves with grace, find meaning in the mundane, and do the disciplines that will develop right desires.

It's a Love Story

You know what kept me going whenever I messed up? Whenever I fell back into a sinful cycle after steering clear from it? Not the disciplines alone, although they kept me safe in the boundaries God gave me. It was the *love* of Christ. The *grace* of God. His *compassion*. The never-ending, always abounding, daily-delivered *mercy* of the Father, our Father.

I do not want to discredit or discount the importance of discipline, of distinct boundaries; I've spent countless chapters hyping up just how effective and crucial they are in the Christian life! However, I do not want you to think that discipline *alone* will help you endure until you see victories in your life. The love of God is the central foundation of this—experiencing and believing in that love as well as reciprocating it. Discipline involves *what* we are doing, but the love, grace, compassion, and mercy of God are *why* and *how* we keep moving forward when we fall.

He loves you.

I know you've heard it said, read it in the Bible, and nodded as people mentioned it in conversations. Please sit with this; meditate on this truth:

The one true, perfect God, who is all good, just, mighty, and sovereign, sees you. Knows you. Loves you. In spite of knowing everything you've done wrong, are presently doing, and will eventually do. He doesn't give up on you. He chooses you. He wants to father you and befriend you. He knows who you are, who He has called and created you to be. He can bring life into what's dead and purpose in place of pain. He wants to be your strength. He wants to love your broken pieces back together. He wants to restore you and heal you for as long as it takes, because He is patient and understands why you do what you don't want to. He walks with you, sits with you, and desires so greatly to take care of you. He is so beautiful—the most beautiful—yet He declares you His beloved. He wants nothing but the best for you, what will give you the most fulfilling life. He is real. He is near. Better yet, He is here. He is in the room with you right now. In the car. On the plane. He is everywhere. He shows up when you call on His name and beckons your heart to be still and know Him.

To know Him is to love Him and to love Him is to truly live. To love Him is to live for Him, to reject anything carnal that threatens to destroy you or to tear you away from the world's one true Love. To love Him is to return to Him. He loves you and waits with open arms, ready to receive you. He never turns His back on you. It's never too late.

Today is the day of salvation.

Today is the day for change.

Today is the day for freedom.

He is there, has always been there, and always will be there.

He is I AM.

Remember, Practice Makes Permanent

We are taking steps in the right direction, a new direction, in redeeming our desires before the Lord. Freedom is a promise given to us, promoted by our discipline and God's love. We need both to be sustained and to run the race well. Here are some truths we shouldn't forget as we develop new disciplines and desires in our walk with Christ:

- Discipline is not enough to sustain you, but God's love is. Our discipline, effort, and work is half the equation, but a genuine and active relationship with God will fan the flame and keep the fire burning within us, refining us every step of the way.

- Devotion to the things of God requires us to draw a line in the sand. We need a firm boundary we are not willing to compromise. The second we begin to entertain thoughts of *Maybe I can do this just one more time*, we need to put the idea to death. Any compromising thought or situation needs a boundary to dispel the temptation that encourages us to enter dangerous and dark territory.

- Don't give up just because you fail. You are not defined by your mistakes. You are not a failure. You are defined by God, and because of Christ you share in His victory. You can get back up from a fall; Christ will heal you and help you run the race He has called you to. He will not leave you in the dust or make you start over. He has grace for you right here, right now, to keep going and growing as He sanctifies you. Everyday practice leads to permanent change. Consistency is the goal, not perfection.

- Determine what discipline you need to implement in your life today. Just one. Take your time integrating it into everyday life and focus on cultivating it instead of hyper-fixating on ending a bad habit. Consume your mind with the ways of Christ.

CHAPTER TWELVE

RUNNING THE RACE BY HIS GOODNESS AND GRACE

Back in 2017, I went on a mission trip to Italy. I know, not a bad place to preach the gospel! From the beautiful Merano mountains to the flowing channels of Venice, it was one of the most life-changing trips I've ever been on. Leading up to our outreach trip, we were preparing our hearts for the street evangelism we were going to do. Evangelism is when believers share the gospel and Christianity through preaching and sharing their testimonies. In the months and weeks prior to boarding the plane, I had felt the Holy Spirit convicting me to surrender a few things to Him. I was not fully obeying and trusting Him in some areas, and I had been delaying His call to surrender. Holding on to these things overwhelmed my heart with restlessness, and when I couldn't take it anymore, I obeyed God. I let go of everything, and He instantly filled me with peace, relief, and comfort. It's sometimes hard to let go of people, patterns, and ways of thinking, to trust God when you don't know the outcome. But on that trip I wanted to serve God wholeheartedly, and that required obedience in everything.

Laying It All Down

While in deep prayer at a worship night the evening before our first day of outreach, I had an unforgettable, amazing God encounter. I couldn't deny it—He was speaking truly and directly to my spirit. There were no goosebumps, no forced emotions, no fakery—just legitimate and intimate communication. Like that of my salvation encounter, it ranked as one of the most real experiences of my life, and rightly so—God is the most real person in existence.

He spoke to my spirit directly and told me, *Keep up with My pace and keep your eyes fixed on Me, because we're about to run a race. Step where I step and go where I go. You have to keep up.* God clearly convicted my soul: He was about to usher in some God-ordained opportunities, and I didn't want to miss a beat. Not because I didn't want to "miss my blessing"; I simply wanted to be where He was. His presence is the safest, most joyful, assuring place to be. I surrendered something to Him that was not good for me, and in exchange, He began to unravel His plans and purposes for my life. Running the race and doing life with Jesus requires our willingness to abandon anything He asks us to lay down: the good, the bad, and the ugly . . . including the habits that comfort us.

We are no longer moseying on the side of the road, kicking rocks, picking daisies, and chilling on the sidelines. God has called *you* to a specific path, the narrow path, and if you are going to fit on it, you have to remove whatever clutters your life. I have never run a marathon, and I don't plan on it. My knees are too injured from my competitive cheerleading days. But I do know that runners dress light. They don't want anything pushing against the wind to hold them back; they throw off every hindrance to go faster, go farther, and get to that goal. We need that same mindset and conviction in living for Christ. Are we willing to throw off what hinders so we can go further, faster in the will of God?

From the First Step to the Finish Line

During the times of Jesus and the New Testament, known as antiquity, athletic events were very popular—just like they are today. That is why the author of Hebrews used this analogy in his plea to believers to remain steadfast, living a life completely dedicated to God's will:

Therefore, since we are surrounded by such a great cloud of witnesses, let us throw off everything that hinders and the sin that so easily entangles. And let us run with perseverance the race marked out for us, fixing our eyes on Jesus, the pioneer and perfecter of faith. For the joy set before him he endured the cross, scorning its shame, and sat down at the right hand of the throne of God. Consider him who endured such opposition from sinners, so that you will not grow weary and lose heart. (12:1–3)

And the apostle Paul wrote in 1 Corinthians 9:24–27,

Do you not know that in a race all the runners run, but only one gets the prize? Run in such a way as to get the prize. Everyone who competes in the games goes into strict training. They do it to get a crown that will not last, but we do it to get a crown that will last forever. Therefore I do not run like someone running aimlessly; I do not fight like a boxer beating the air. No, I strike a blow to my body and make it my slave so that after I have preached to others, I myself will not be disqualified for the prize.

Our life is short. It is one long, final stretch to the finish line. We want to run the race and finish it well. Perhaps you've been running with ankle weights that make it hard to lift those legs and keep moving forward. Maybe you've stuffed some things in your backpack that tire you out so you can't run full force. Whatever is clinging to you—an addiction, a battle against sexual immorality, self-harming your body, gossip and slander, bitterness and explosions of anger, coveting and envy, or a myriad of other habitual sins—*it can be removed*. The second you allow Christ to lead and you begin to follow His instruction, you'll find it easier to strip away those pesky weights clinging to you, the ones that drag you down. So chug that pre-workout fuel, lace up your sneakers, strap on that smartwatch to track those steps. Get ready, get set, go!

Infants Aren't Track Stars, and Neither Am I

As we assume the starting position for our race, some of us may shoot off into a full sprint as soon as we hear the gunshot. Don't get me wrong: zeal is beautiful and passion is admirable, but a sprint isn't sustainable for the entire journey. It will require endurance, good pacing, focus, and maturity. Like a spiritual baby, we must learn first to crawl, and then mature into full-on, long-lasting mobility as our muscles and joints grow in strength.

When we decide we're ready to throw away the former things and run after Jesus, it feels great! We have drive, passion, inspiration, zeal, and conviction. We want to be victorious and overcome whatever burdens hold us back, but then come the hurdles. Yeah, we aren't just running the race; we are also jumping hurdles on this narrow path. Perhaps we aren't fully prepared; we still struggle with certain temptations or we get burned out along the way; we hit the hurdle and fall. That crash with the obstacle before us may feel like failure, as though our whole world is crashing down around us.

When I failed after doing well for a while, I often fell into a hopeless headspace, and that's where the Enemy wanted me—to refuse to believe I could ever recover from my mistakes, that all my efforts were in vain, and I should just give up. Maybe I sound dramatic, but maybe you do this too! Maybe that is *exactly* how you feel, and you just want to crawl into your bed and cry. I've had many nights where I just wanted to curl up, weep, and sleep, so it could be tomorrow already; the failures of that day were enough to defeat and define me.

Friend, you and I both need to get out of that headspace, out of that bed, and off the sidelines. Do you honestly think that someone running hurdles the first time will do it perfectly? Of course not! We cheer on professionally trained athletes in the Olympics, but what do you think their first round of training looked like? Probably like us at first. It takes time, training, discipline, effort, and a rejection of defeat, a spirit that gets back up and tries again, that knows even the failures propel us forward. We learn from our mistakes, we grow from the trials and the run-throughs, and we progress when we choose to keep going. We don't have to hit the hurdle and stay on the ground; we can get back up and do better the next time.

> **WE LEARN FROM OUR MISTAKES, WE GROW FROM THE TRIALS AND THE RUN-THROUGHS, AND WE PROGRESS WHEN WE CHOOSE TO KEEP GOING.**

Scripture tells us in 2 Timothy 2:22 to "run from anything that stimulates youthful lusts. Instead, pursue righteous living, faithfulness, love, and peace. Enjoy the companionship of those who call on the Lord with pure hearts" (NLT). God calls us to run toward many things and face them head-on. We will have to deal with our sin and put it in its place. This is true for fear, harbored anger, resentment, unforgiveness, jealousy, comparison, insecurity, and the like. Some of us, most I assume, need to simply cut ties with certain sin and run in the other direction in repentance. The ones that stick out to me the most are sexual sin and lust. Paul wrote in 1 Corinthians 6:18, "Flee sexual immorality. Every sin that a man does is outside the body, but he who commits sexual immorality sins against his own body" (NKJV). Sexual sin harms you in different ways from other sins, but that does not make it any worse than any other sin. We need to deal with unforgiveness as badly as a porn addiction, with anger as much as promiscuity, with gossip and slander as much as adultery. We all need help, we all need healing, and we all need Jesus to save us and help us run this race with no chains binding us.

Life Alert vs. the Lifeline

Do you remember those old Life Alert commercials from the early 2000s with elderly people lying across the floor yelling, "Help! I've fallen and I can't get up!"? Some of us have felt this way for a long time. Vulnerable, frail, unequipped, and prone to falling. I don't mean to sound cheesy, but Jesus is like Life Alert. We can call on Him and get the assistance we need when we fall. He'll get us back up on our feet and ensure we're okay to keep moving forward. But Jesus is so much more than a Life Alert. He is our *lifeline*. He daily walks with us, stabilizes our steps, directs us, and shows us how to grow in wisdom, stature, and favor, like He did (Luke 2:52). We don't have to lie on the ground helpless anymore!

Hebrews 12:1–2 says, "Therefore, since we are surrounded by so great a cloud of witnesses, let us also lay aside every weight, and sin which clings so closely, and let us run with endurance the race that is set before us, looking to Jesus, the founder and perfecter of our faith, who for the joy that was set before him endured the cross, despising the shame, and is seated at the right hand of the throne of God" (ESV). The reality of sin is that it clings so closely to us. It does all it can to dig its sharp nails into our heels, drag us down, or drag us along as we try to advance in our faith. It feels so discouraging to continue to wrestle and revisit areas we thought we had escaped or hoped we'd be free from at this point. Unfortunately, the church might have failed to teach us something.

What Every Christian Needs to Know

Some churches (not all) have failed in discipling Christians well, especially newer believers. Fortunately, I never had extensive pressure to "never sin again" or "be perfect, or else God might disown me." I fully understood my sin as disobedience toward God and harmful to me and my relationship with God, and I never took my shortcomings lightly. However, I think many of us have not been taught that the Christian walk is a *lifelong journey*, requiring a lifelong process of sanctification. God changes us to mature in our walk with Jesus and look more like Him. It's like archaeologists at a dig, shoveling up dirt and using their tools to reveal the artifacts, the treasure, beneath. All of this takes careful, intentional time. It's the same for us and our walk with Jesus. To get to what has always been underneath, that which Christ is calling out of us, we have to let Him dig away, chip at, and dust off the old bits and pieces hiding who we will become in Him.

Maturity does not develop overnight. Think about puberty (yeah, I know, the most awkward example ever). You did not develop into a fully matured individual overnight, physically or mentally. Not all our sinful desires will fade away in an instant. Most often, it takes time as we develop. A desire for Christ, a deeper understanding of God's character and truth, and the Holy Spirit's conviction and revelation in our lives will help us completely abandon the elementary ways that pale in comparison to God.

Lane Adams once said, "Friend, there is no such thing as instant maturity. I know of no shortcuts whatsoever in the realm of spiritual growth."[1] You cannot manufacture or mass-produce spiritual growth and maturity. That only comes from quality time spent with Jesus. I know you so badly want to be five years down the road in your maturation process, but there is so much beauty in showing up daily, laying down your old desires, inviting God in, and relying on Him every step of the way. This not only brings you out of the pit and into freedom but teaches intimacy and a knowing of Jesus you wouldn't have without firsthand experience. There is no spiritual dupe for sanctification. Only the real thing will prepare and sustain you for this race. It requires endurance and steadfastness (Hebrews 10:35–36; James 1:12).

Maybe a mentor, a pastor, some church elders, or volunteers put an unnecessary amount of pressure on you to follow rules to earn God's love, or they claimed if you messed up, it meant you weren't really saved. On behalf of them, I am so sorry they did that. God has so much mercy and grace for you. Yes, He wants to free you from sin and does not want you actively living a life of sin, but He is so gentle in the sanctification process. He kindly holds your hand as you walk out healing and restoration. God is truly good, like *actually* so considerate and good to us. He is a loving Father who cares for His children. He will never fail you as you get up and walk the narrow path He calls you to. He will help free you of those burdens, desires, and habits, the old fleshly ways that cling so tightly. You can run the race anew with nothing holding you back. It just takes time. Be patient. Be faithful. Just show up today and let Him grow you inch by inch, day by day.

Getting Good at Jumping over Your Hurdles

It was no walk in the park overcoming my habitual struggle against pornography. It did not happen overnight. There were times when I had the strength and discipline to resist temptation and see another day of victory, but there were also days when I gave in to temptation. Over time, it became easier to call out Satan when I saw a foul play and see my sin for what it truly was. It started to become so unappealing as I immersed myself in the truth of God and a genuine relationship with Jesus.

I became very proactive in avoiding the obstacle: anything that would tempt me in a lustful way. This looked like deleting certain apps, choosing certain settings on my devices, and implementing boundaries and strict disciplines like turning off my electronics at certain times or using a university computer instead of my own. This may seem extreme, but sin has some serious side effects. We must treat this deathly illness with extensive care and "antibiotics." I am reminded of Jesus' words to His disciples in Matthew 18:7–9:

> "Woe to the world for temptations to sin! For it is necessary that temptations come, but woe to the one by whom the temptation comes! And if your hand or your foot causes you to sin, cut it off and throw it away. It is better for you to enter life crippled or lame than with two hands or two feet to be thrown into the eternal fire. And if your eye causes you to sin, tear it out and throw it away. It is better for you to enter life with one eye than with two eyes to be thrown into the hell of fire." (ESV)

Is this passage telling us to literally cut off our limbs and gouge out our eyes because we don't want to end up in hell for our sins? No. Jesus is using exaggerated language here. He means that if anything is causing you to stumble—whether you are reaching for and handling it, wandering after it, gazing upon it, or otherwise—you need to remove that obstacle from your vicinity. There should be no point of contact. You shouldn't be able to grab it and reach for it, walk toward it, or view it. It is better for me to lock and put my phone away at night so my hand doesn't reach for it and my eyes don't gaze upon things I should not be viewing. These verses stress the importance of taking measures, the doable and the drastic, to make sure the sin that so easily entangles us doesn't tread near the boundaries we have established.

I think of those old-time castles with huge moats and draw-bridges around them. We not only want fortified city walls to protect us on the inside, but we should go as far as digging moats around us, filling them with alligators and piranhas, and closing our drawbridge so no enemies can successfully creep their way in. We must take intentional action and serious measures to protect our minds, bodies, eyes, ears, and souls from the things of the Enemy.

I also proactively called out temptations when they came. When those temptations and desires begin to rise within you, it almost feels like someone puts sound-canceling headphones on you and slowly turns up the music louder and louder until you can't take it anymore. You do whatever silences it to satisfy your flesh, leaving you empty, ashamed, and disappointed. Once I finally confessed and exposed my sin, I called it out the moment I felt that urge, temptation, or desire make its way into my day. Oftentimes, I would audibly say, "No. I am not doing this. I see you and know what you are, and I am not doing it."

That might sound silly, but sin is not silly. It's destructive. It's divisive. It's dehumanizing. It's disappointing. Sin is not worth it and is never enough. It consumes and crushes. Call it out! Literally, call it out in your life. "Hey, you [insert specific habitual sin here]! You need to leave. I am not doing this. I refuse to cooperate. I do not want to do this, I do not agree with your terms and conditions, I will not give you any time or territory in my life, and you have to leave in Jesus' name." You'd be surprised how calling out sin turns into calling upon the name of the Lord, transitioning into prayer and petition, and declaring the truth of God over the lies and attacks of the Enemy. Calling it out and asking for the power, deliverance, and strength of God enables you to dismiss its attempts at attacking your peace, sanity, and sanctity.

My third proactive tactic involves seeing sin for what it is. Take the example of my struggle against pornography. I decided I wanted to learn the truth behind the porn industry. I was completely astounded and disgusted at how the industry dehumanizes people, destroys relationships and marriages, feeds into abuse and the demand for sex trafficking, and skews safe intimacy in relationships. I won't get into all the facts, but if you want to see it for what it truly is, I encourage you to look up the site Fight the New Drug and view its resources. Also check out my good friend Joshua Broome, who has an incredible testimony of God redeeming him from the porn industry. Once I realized the ugliness and destruction behind my sin, I could never see it the same way again. God shattered my rose-colored glasses, and my appetite for that sin started to fizzle out. The realities of addiction, gossip, sleeping around, substance abuse, fits of rage, pride, divisiveness, greed, and every other sin out there are revolting when you peel back the curtain and examine how harmful they are to you and others. They look delightful in the dark, but when exposed in the light, they leave you with a sour taste.

Paul, who called himself the "chief of sinners," also wrote, "No temptation has overtaken you except what is common to mankind. And God is faithful; he will not let you be tempted beyond what you can bear. But when you are tempted, he will also provide a way out so that you can endure it" (1 Corinthians 10:13). Perhaps right now you feel like God has allowed you to carry an impossible burden, to jump over the highest hurdle, to endure the most impossible trial. That is 100% how I felt at the time. I never believed I could overcome that temptation. I was so deceived by the devil, thinking it was always something I would struggle with and succumb to. I thought that verse was for everyone besides me. Man, oh man, was I wrong! As I matured in my faith, grew in my love for the Word of God and God Himself, and began to see sin clearly, I was empowered to hop the hurdles that once stood in my way of freedom.

BATTLE PLAN STEP #11:
Be Proactive

When we reveal sin for what it is and clearly see the obstacles ahead, the race isn't so scary to run. God will give us the strength, endurance, and ability to hop over hurdles and overcome any adversity that stands between us and where He calls us to go. Let's summarize what we just read:

- As we get ready to run the race, we must be willing to cast off every weight, burden, and distraction when Christ convicts us. It isn't always easy to surrender things to God that feel comfortable or we're attached to, but His ways are always better. He will reveal His will and purposes in time; for now, be obedient and embrace the coming journey.

- As we prepare to run the race, we mustn't hold ourselves to the standard of spiritual Olympians just yet. We are doing something new; we will be infants in it. The Lord will strengthen us, mature us, and teach us how to run. He will faithfully train and equip us for every good work He calls us to as we run faithfully as well. Don't compare your walk, or run, to others. Keep your eyes on the true prize: Jesus.

- We need to know that Jesus is readily available to help us at any given moment. Like a Life Alert, He will help us when we fall and can't get back up. He is also a healer—the Great Physician—a friend when we get knocked down. Do not be afraid to call on Him for rescue; He is your Savior!

- Let's proactively ready ourselves for the obstacles ahead. We need to avoid areas that trip us up, call out temptation the second we see it, and see our sin for what it is: disorderly and destructive. As we do this, sin will begin to lose its appeal and its grip on us.

CHAPTER THIRTEEN

THERE IS HOPE AHEAD

Friend, I have so much hope for you, the steps you will take, and the choices you will make. As excited and expectant as I am for the testimonies to rejoice alongside that may come from this book, you need to know what to expect once you close the cover.

I 100% guarantee that you will run into problems, struggles, and temptations—maybe even new ones you never thought you'd face—once you put to death desires previously running rampant in your life. We have to be honest with ourselves about our sinful world and our sinful selves (despite our ongoing sanctification). We cannot pretend we will not struggle or face difficulties from this moment on. We need to be aware of ourselves, the disobedience and flesh within us, the Enemy prowling around us, and the obstacles the world will throw our way that we will either overcome or trip over. Spiritual warfare is real, and the Enemy is willing, ready, and aiming to fire at us right this instant. How should we respond? Let's learn from the laws of warfare in Deuteronomy.

The Battle Is Inevitable

> When you go out to war against your enemies, and see horses and chariots and an army larger than your own, you shall not be afraid of them, for the LORD your God is with you, who brought you up out of the land of Egypt. And when you draw near to the battle, the priest shall come forward and speak to the people and shall say to them, "Hear, O Israel, today you are drawing near for battle against your enemies: let not your heart faint. Do not fear or panic or be in dread of them, for the LORD your God is he who goes with you to fight for you against your enemies, to give you the victory." (Deuteronomy 20:1–4 ESV)

I love this collection of verses. Even from the first few words— *when* you go to war—I am amazed. That singular word, *when*, shows that the battle is inevitable! The people of God are warriors. Whether it is on an actual field or within our flesh, we are at war against something or someone: Satan, the *real* Enemy.

How are the people of God called to respond to the coming war? Let's condense the simple instructions listed above: we are not to be afraid, then we face the battle, remember the truth about who our God is, not be faint of heart (lacking courage to face something dangerous), not panic over our opposition, and remember that even as we fight, the Lord goes before us and fights on our behalf.

One Day at a Time

My father was an addict. He struggled with alcoholism his entire adult life, and it eventually killed him when I was just ten years old. Back in 2019, I got to visit my dad's side of the family in New Jersey and read through some of his old letters, look through his old photos, and riffle through memorabilia my nana had kept. I came across a private letter he had written to his aunt, and for the first time as a young adult, I saw a side of my father that I never knew as a young child. I peeked behind the curtain to see his struggle with the habit that led to my parents' divorce, the loss of his job, other sinful lifestyle choices, and eventually his death.

In this letter, he explained how hard it was to break his habit of excessive drinking, but he knew it was possible. He couldn't focus on sobriety a month, a year, or five years from then; that was too much pressure to bear considering how dependent his body had become on alcohol just to function normally. He learned in Alcoholics Anonymous that the only way he could sober up and rehabilitate was to take it *one day at a time*. That's it. One day at a time. Friend, with the support of a healthy and loving community, the assistance and advice of addiction specialists and rehabilitation professionals, the help of medical experts and spiritual mentors, and our willing reliance on Jesus' strength and freeing power, we, too, can face addiction with hope and confidence that we can be free. It is a *daily* decision that we can make; one that can impact our entire lives and the lives of those around us. Even though my dad's life ended so suddenly, cut short by a destructive habit, your life doesn't have to. You can live out your life boldly for Christ, in freedom, one day at a time.

Your hope, your joy, your future, and your freedom do not have to be stolen from you. Your only obligation right now? To wake up and decide how you will live on this day: *Will I serve the Lord, or will I satisfy my flesh?* You get to wake up in the morning and choose how to spend your next moment; I encourage you to commit and surrender it all to the Lord. We cannot do it without His help! You don't need to worry: *What if I fail tomorrow or next week? What if I have another three-month winning streak but fall on the fourth?* Get that worry out of your mind; tell it to Jesus, then refocus on your next small step. As Philippians 4 explains: God cares for you, He cares about you, and He cares about what you care about. He will provide for your needs today and forever because He cares about you.

My mom was an addict too. She also struggled with alcoholism, and in the spring of 2023, she passed away due to complications it unfortunately nurtured. Her body was not strong enough to pull through without the help of life support. She had battled this addiction throughout her adult life as well, but here was the difference I observed in her that I sadly did not see in my father. She chose Christ daily. Even on the days she picked up a drink instead of a Bible, she did her absolute best to battle the beast of addiction and put her hope in Christ. Her sin had major consequences in her untimely death, but I know that toward the end of my beloved mother's life, she had a beautiful relationship with God. She always prayed for God's guidance, direction, and strength to lead her in her weakness, because apart from Him she knew she could not do it. Though I wish these were not the circumstances of her life's end,

I know she is now with Jesus, totally free in His presence from all the pain, sickness, and sin of this world.

I am all the more encouraged to carry the torch in our family that leads others out of darkness, into freedom. I pick up my Bible instead of a bottle to cope with the hard realities of life, and I choose to abandon what the Enemy uses to steal, kill, and destroy us. I invite you to join me on the front line—to stand firm for yourself, your family, your friends, your significant other, your coworker, your neighbor, and for the Lord. Sin has taken too many people captive, and freedom will begin with us, for our own sake, and for the sake of current and future generations. We can be the change. We can be the ones who usher in freedom and trailblaze it in our communities!

Let's Be Still for a Moment

As we begin to wrap things up, I want us to meditate on the words David wrote in Psalm 103. Allow them to take root in your heart. Be still and take this in verse by verse, without any rushing or skimming.

> Let all that I am praise the LORD;
>> with my whole heart, I will praise his
>>> holy name.
> Let all that I am praise the LORD;
>> may I never forget the good things he does
>>> for me.
> He forgives all my sins
>> and heals all my diseases.

He redeems me from death
 and crowns me with love and tender mercies.
He fills my life with good things.
 My youth is renewed like the eagle's!

The LORD gives righteousness
 and justice to all who are treated unfairly.

He revealed his character to Moses
 and his deeds to the people of Israel.
The LORD is compassionate and merciful,
 slow to get angry and filled with
  unfailing love.
He will not constantly accuse us,
 nor remain angry forever.
He does not punish us for all our sins;
 he does not deal harshly with us, as
  we deserve.
For his unfailing love toward those who
  fear him
 is as great as the height of the heavens
  above the earth.
He has removed our sins as far from us
 as the east is from the west.
The LORD is like a father to his children,
 tender and compassionate to those who
  fear him.
For he knows how weak we are;
 he remembers we are only dust.
Our days on earth are like grass;

like wildflowers, we bloom and die.
The wind blows, and we are gone—
    as though we had never been here.
But the love of the L ORD remains forever
    with those who fear him.
His salvation extends to the children's children
    of those who are faithful to his covenant,
    of those who obey his commandments!

The L ORD has made the heavens his throne;
    from there he rules over everything.

Praise the L ORD, you angels,
    you mighty ones who carry out his plans,
    listening for each of his commands.
Yes, praise the L ORD, you armies of angels
    who serve him and do his will!
Praise the L ORD, everything he has created,
    everything in all his kingdom.

Let all that I am praise the L ORD. (NLT)

I Believe in Your Freedom

Honestly, I never imagined I could be truly free from what was
holding me back and weighing me down. That sin I was stuck in?
That cycle I could not seem to break out of? I didn't even dare to
dream of freedom, because it seemed so far out of reach, knowing
just how defeated I was. But Jesus, our Savior, reaches into the pit

to pull us up, into the waters to rescue us from drowning, off the ground where we've been knocked down. He shakes off the dust that's clouded our vision far too long. He was my helping hand, and the hand I've continued to hold as I've made my way through life. To this day, I am firmly holding His righteous right hand, experiencing daily deliverance, protection, and peace.

Temptation came. Temptation *still* comes. I have stumbled. I *still* mess up. I have made mistakes. But I have also *overcome*. I've said no. I've denied my flesh and seen old desires wither away as my love for God and His goodness grows. I continue to get back up when a new temptation comes, and I go to war to squash it under my feet. His love for me has sustained me, and my love for Him has maintained me, when every other effort failed.

I can gladly say that I have been porn-free for over seven years. Even as I type this out, I can't believe it! Actually . . . I can! Because my God is just that good, His Word is just that true, and His promises are that attainable. Temptation took a while to subside, but even on those long evenings when I felt weak, I was able to push through because I relied on God, recalled His truth, recited it, and remembered the reality of the Enemy and the life Jesus gave me.

I am speaking from the other side of this journey, telling you that it is possible. That you don't have to live in defeat or cut your life short. You have life to live, and full, abundant life is found in Jesus! I have found it, I am free in it, and I've got to say, it is the best place ever. I can't wait to have you join me here on the other side of your obstacle!

Remember that it's not just about doing better, praying harder, having "more faith," or dismissing the root of the issue. It's about knowing, believing, trusting, and loving God. We have to acknowledge our sin and our need for a Savior. When we truly understand things for what they are, the clarity helps us see what we've been falling for and who we should be following instead.

Sin doesn't have to rule our lives anymore; our God reigns! Temptation doesn't have to dictate our destiny any longer; our God delivers! In the front seat of my journey, I see where He has me, living with desires and convictions that agree with His Word and spur me closer toward His heart. I know this can be true in your life too! I am nowhere near perfect, but Christ is perfecting me every day to love Him more and my flesh less. To look like Him more and my old self less. Just like you, in Christ I am redeemed, I am set free, I am loved, I am empowered, I am strengthened, I am encouraged, and I am able.

Bring Out the Battle Plan

When you submit your daily decisions to His direction, guidance, and commands, you will have the best strategy in the world for facing the next temptation that comes your way. Don't be surprised if the Enemy throws a curveball when you put this book down, because he knows you're a threat to his kingdom of darkness if you're on the front lines of God's kingdom. Every day, you get to decide that you will do what God's Word empowers you to. You don't have to bow down to

> WHEN YOU SUBMIT YOUR DAILY DECISIONS TO HIS DIRECTION, GUIDANCE, AND COMMANDS, YOU WILL HAVE THE BEST STRATEGY IN THE WORLD FOR FACING THE NEXT TEMPTATION THAT COMES YOUR WAY.

the Enemy's taunts any longer. God has authority over you, not our defeated enemy. Remember, we fight *from* victory and *for* victory!

Our obedience will lead us to overcome. It takes a combination of our decisions and dependency on the Lord's strength to daily choose God's will for our life and nurture our relationship with Him. Take everything you now know from the battle plan we've formed about God, our enemy, and how we function as humans, and apply it to live in obedience to God by understanding His truth and love.

You can face today, tomorrow, and every day with knowledge, awareness, and strategy for when the deceiver, the destroyer, the devil shoots his flaming darts at you. This time, they don't have to stick! You don't have to fall back into the mud and muck that once kept you stuck. You can be fully, truly, finally free!

Let's go over this Battle Plan one more time in full, shall we?

Step 1: Connect and Confess

Step 2: Stay in Bounds

Step 3: Know Your Enemy

Step 4: Know Your God

Step 5: Know Yourself

Step 6: Set Your Green- and Red-Light Zones

Step 7: Turn Around and Come Home

Step 8: Let Go and Look Ahead

Step 9: Make Over Your Mind

Step 10: Remember Practice Makes Permanent

Step 11: Be Proactive

And one final step I want to commission you with:

Step 12: BE FREE!

I now hand the hard work over to you. Now it's your turn to obey, get to work, and leave behind what's been buried in the grave, to walk in the freedom and fullness of life in Christ, forever changed. You can be free!

Please, never be afraid to come back to this book when you need help, hope, encouragement, and guidance as you ward off sin, whether old temptations resurface or you face a new one. I hope you first run to and envelop yourself in God and the Bible, but know that this book will always serve as a cheerleader in your corner too.

I believe in your freedom. I believe the truth that God can do all things! He can heal, restore, redeem, empower, forgive, and break off your chains, like only a Savior could do. This is Jesus, for goodness' sake: He conquered the grave! Don't underestimate what He can do in you and through you, especially as you set your eyes on freedom. You've got this. Get to it, friend!

ACKNOWLEDGMENTS

I want to honor a few individuals here at the end of my first book. I hope you take a moment to read this to see the amazing influence and impact poured into this book that ministered to you.

I first and foremost want to honor my mother, Susan Christine Minnick, who passed away May 18, 2023, just as I was sending off the final edits of this book. I wish she'd gotten to read it and see this dream of mine come to fruition. My mother had her fair share of struggles against addiction and habitual sin, and though the Lord allowed her time on this earth to end suddenly, I know she is finally fully free in His presence. She no longer has to suffer, and though I wish she could have overcome everything she was enduring, she had the hope of Christ. Her soul was free from the condemnation of sin, and she knew how much my family and the Lord loved her. In honor of her, I pray God will use this book to set someone free from their addiction, and that they go on to live a changed life of freedom and boldness, sharing how Jesus set them free by His power. I love you, Mama Bear. This book was always meant for your hands.

Second, to Richard, my incredibly loving husband. Richard, you have my whole heart. You love me with such a pure, selfless, and strong love that lifts me up when I am down, encourages me when I feel defeated, and comforts me when I am at my weakest. You are my better half, and I am so grateful that God gave me a man like you to lead me and love me in the ways of Christ. You so graciously exemplify Him to everyone around you daily, and this book couldn't have been written without your support. Because of you, I understand the grace and forgiveness of God far greater, and truly believe that anyone and everyone is worthy in the eyes of God. Nobody is too far gone, not even a sinner like me. Thank you for seeing me how Christ sees me. I love you.

To the incredible individuals, family, and friends who hosted my husband and me on my writing retreats, I want to thank you, beginning with Grandpa Doyle and his wife, Mary. Thank you for believing in me and believing in this book. You were the first ones who made arrangements for Richard and me to visit and set up a writing retreat—it set the stage for this book to come to life. I am grateful not only for the time and space to work there but for the quality time and memories I made with you both while visiting after my intense writing sessions. I love you both enormously, and I am blessed to have you as family.

To our second hosts, Haley Pham and Ryan Trahan, thank you for opening your home to Richard and me so I could get away and work on this book. You are so giving and gracious, and I am beyond thankful that I have experienced your friendship over social media and in person. You both are huge blessings to my husband and me and to the world. I pray the Lord continues to grant favor and guidance over your lives as you bring joy to the world and bless those who follow as you lead with the example of Christ.

ACKNOWLEDGMENTS

To our third hosts, Jefferson and Alyssa Bethke, you guys rock! It's not every day you get to hop on a plane to Hawaii for a writing retreat at the home of two powerhouse preachers and authors. Richard and I had such a refreshing and fun time with your family, and I felt so encouraged to approach this book with fresh direction and advice. You both helped me to understand the voice of an author even better, and because of that, I am sure the readers can thank you for much of my storytelling. I look up to you both so much, and I am honored that I get to call you friends and mentors. Aloha, mahalo, and long live Jeff's pizza-craze phase!

To my final host, Aaron Marshall, thank you for being such a hospitable person. Thanks to our mutual friend Gareth Pon, I got to fly out with Richard and Jana, my friend and ministry sister, to stay on your beautiful property in Hawaii and finish the final edits of this book. You are seriously one of the sweetest and most creative people I have met, and your home not only provided me with the creative space to refine this book for my readers but also to heal and grieve after the loss of my mother. That is a gift not many people could give. Thank you, friend. I pray that Jesus would continue to reveal His goodness to you and use you for great things!

I want to recognize the youth pastor who discipled me when I first came to the faith, who helped me to shape and test my beliefs, and who serves as a father figure to me—Jared Lyons, and his incredible wife, Ali. I am so glad you noticed me at youth group and helped fan the flame within me. You gave me opportunities to lead, to preach, to walk out my gifts and my calling. You both were there for me in my darkest moments, when I felt most alone and helpless. You were a father and a mother to me when I needed it and friends and mentors when I needed that too. This book wouldn't have been possible without your incredible intentionality in discipling me and helping me to know the way, the truth, and the life. This book, and my confidence and direction in ministry, wouldn't have been possible without your faithfulness. I love you both and your incredible kiddos so dearly!

To CJ, I want to thank you for being another father figure present in the life of my brother and me and for loving my mom amid her addiction. You truly showed her so much unconditional love, and my brother and I needed that example growing up. This book is not only my work but a legacy dedicated to my mom, whom we both love and miss. Thank you for being present to this day in our lives, and for always showing up for the smallest things. I am grateful this is another achievement I can share with you, and I pray it is a blessing to you. I love you!

To DJ, my first friend and big brother! I know I got very real in this book, but I wanted to take a moment to honor and acknowledge the impact you've had on my life. Because of you, life is more fun. Because of you, I understand more of compassion and empathy, and loving everyone no matter the circumstances. Though we don't always have the words to say, I love you more than you could ever know, and I am grateful that I get to be your sister. Because of who you are, I am who I am. I am so grateful that God made you *you*!

I have many friends I want to thank as well for their encouragement and support over the years through the trials and obstacles I mentioned in this book, as well as for the making of this book. I want to acknowledge and express my love and thanks to Elizabeth Wilson, Ashley Rose, Olivia Maxie, Hannah Adeoye, Emily Standerfer, Tara Sun, Nadia Van Dyke, Joe Navarro, Amanda and Michael Pittman, Chelsea and Nick Hurst, Kyrah and Kaelin Edwards, Jasmine and Josh Pernell, Bailey and Jacob Nwangwa, and Julia and Jacob Petersen.

My love for God and knowledge of Him wouldn't be where it is today without Dallas Baptist University and its amazing staff and professors. DBU president Adam Wright, thank you for seeing the gifts God put in me and making a way for me to thrive in my educational career. You've always been so intentional to help students in need and cultivate an environment where students like me could thrive vocationally and ministerially. As a woman in ministry, I thank you so much for affirming God's call on me and checking in to see what He is up to in my life. I wouldn't be where I am today without your leadership and mentorship.

I also want to shout out a few of my favorite and most influential professors. Dr. Jim Lemons, your classes were challenging but taught me so much about the reasoning and foundations of our shared faith. When you became my advisor for graduate school, I was so excited to work with you on mapping out classes and planning my future. The long-awaited book is finally here, and I can't wait for you to read it after our conversations about it. Thank you for believing in me and always going the extra mile to see me succeed. Dr. Brent Thomason, you will always be one of my favorite professors. You birthed within me a joy for researching and diving deeper into theology by asking the hard questions and finding the real answers. Your joy and love for the faith and for scholarship shaped me and shaped this book. Thank you for cheering me on and always taking an interest in God's work through my ministry.

Finally, to Leigh Gettman-Allen, my professor and dear mentor. Where would I be without you? We have shared many laughs and many tears through the years. You have modeled to me what a woman of true integrity and faith looks like. I am so grateful we crossed paths at DBU and that I got to learn under you. That has influenced me to minister in ways that honor people, myself, and God better. You have been a faithful prayer warrior for me, and your motherly spirit has supported me in times when I needed encouragement. We talked about this book in its earliest stages, and I can't wait for you to get to this part.

I love each of you so much!

A huge shout-out to Grant Skeldon for hosting so many amazing Next Gen Retreats that I've had the privilege of attending, because without his ministry and heart for connection, I wouldn't have gotten to know the incredible, trailblazing, powerhouse preacher, speaker, spoken-word artist, and woman of the Lord, Hosanna Wong, who wrote the foreword to this book! Hosanna, I first told you about this book in its beginning stages when nobody knew a thing about it. When we linked up again and you remembered every detail of it, I had to reach out to you for the foreword. Your willingness to read the first draft and commitment to championing it with a foreword means the world to me. You and I both know that this book is not about me. It's about our God whom we love, who has set us free and leads us along the sanctification journey. I am blessed to know you and link arms with you in this way, and I am beyond grateful that you believe in me and God's call on my life as an author, speaker, and woman in ministry. I love you and look up to you, Hosanna. Keep leading and living for Him!

Lastly, to my editing team. (No, they did not add this in here!) Lisa-Jo Baker and Brooke Hill, you two were absolute superstars! This book started one way, and you brought the phrases, stories, and words to life in a more colorful, exciting, relatable way, true

ACKNOWLEDGMENTS

to everything in my heart. Thank you for trusting in me, believing in me, and amplifying my creative voice, not shutting it out. I trust and believe in you both! I especially want you to have the final place of honor, along with my literary agent, Trinity McFadden. All three of you saw this book in me and helped birth it from beginning to end. This first-book dream team has been more than a dream, and I am so happy to celebrate this whole process and treasure it as a genuine joy from beginning to end. I love you three so much!

NOTES

Chapter 2

1. "Fast Facts about Pornography," Fight the New Drug, accessed November 11, 2023, https://fightthenewdrug.org/fast-fact-2/.
2. "Fast Facts about Pornography."

Chapter 3

1. Sun Tzu, *The Art of War* (Leicester, England: Allandale Online Publishing, 2000), 11, https://sites.ualberta.ca/~enoch/Readings/The_Art_Of_War.pdf.

Chapter 4

1. Imagine Dragons, "Demons," 0:55, track 4 on *Night Visions*, KIDinaKORNER/Interscope Records, 2012, iTunes, https://music.apple.com/us/album/demons/1440873107?i=1440873339.
2. Imagine Dragons, "Demons," 0:50.
3. Verses in this paragraph are paraphrased by the author.

Chapter 5

1. *America's Next Top Model*, season 4, episode 7, aired April 13, 2005, written by Tyra Banks, Kenya Barris, and Ken Mok, directed by Tony Croll et al., on UPN.
2. "What Is the Conviction of Sin?" Got Questions, accessed November 11, 2023, https://www.gotquestions.org/conviction-of-sin.html.
3. Charles Caldwell Ryrie, *Basic Theology: A Popular Systematic Guide to Understanding Biblical Truth* (Chicago: Moody Press, 1999), 238–39.
4. "Are There Degrees of Sin?", Making Life Count Ministries, accessed November 11, 2023, https://s3.amazonaws.com/media.cloversites.com/fc/fcdcda31–90dd-4d9e-8256–2b8bc499f91b/documents/Sin-Transgression-Iniquity.pdf; "What Is the Difference Between Iniquity, Sin, and Transgression?" Got Questions, accessed November 11, 2023, https://www.gotquestions.org/iniquity-sin-transgression.html.
5. "What Is the Difference Between Iniquity, Sin, and Transgression?"

Chapter 6

1. Robert Morris, "Simply Human," November 7, 2020, from the sermon series *Perfect or Perfected*, Gateway Church, https://gatewaypeople.com/series/perfect-or-perfected?sermon=simply-human.

Chapter 7

1. Susan Peirce Thompson, *Bright Line Eating: The Science of Living Happy, Thin and Free* (Carlsbad, CA: Hay House, 2017), 26–27.
2. Thompson, *Bright Line Eating*, 118–20.

NOTES

Chapter 8

1. KJV *Bible Dictionary*, s.v. "renounce," https://
kingjamesbibledictionary.com/Dictionary/renounce.
2. The Lexham Bible Dictionary, (Bellingham, WA: Lexham
Press, 2016), s.v. "redemption," https://app.logos.com/books
/LLS%3ALBD/references/bk.%25redemption.
3. *Dictionary of Biblical Imagery* (Downers Grove, IL:
InterVarsity Press, 2000), s.v. "restore, restoration," https://
archive.org/details/dictionary-of-biblical-imagery-ryken
-wilhoit-temper-longman-iii/mode/2up.
4. *Tyndale Bible Dictionary*, (Wheaton, IL: Tyndale House,
2001), s.v. "reconciliation," 1113, accessed November 11,
2023, https://app.logos.com/refly?uri
=logosres%3Atynbibdct%3Bref%3DPage.p_1113%3Boff
%3D4116%3Bctx%3DRECONCILIATION_~Restoration
_of_friendly_r, Logos Bible Study app.

Chapter 9

1. *The Brady Bunch*, season 4, episodes 1–3, "Hawaii
Bound," "Pass the Tabu," and "The Tiki Caves," directed
by Jack Arnold, written by Sherwood Schwartz and Tam
Spiva, aired September 22, 1972; September 29, 1972; and
October 6, 1972, https://www.imdb.com/title/tt0531098/.

Chapter 10

1. Julie Hani, "The Neuroscience of Behavior Change,"
StartUp Health, August 8, 2017, https://healthtransformer.
co/the-neuroscience-of-behavior-change-bcb567fa83c1.
2. Northwestern University Feinberg School of Medicine:
Research, "The Role of Dopamine in Habit Formation
and Compulsive Behavior with Talia Lerner, PhD,"
November 1, 2022, *Breakthroughs* podcast, https://

www.feinberg.northwestern.edu/research/podcast/2022
/role-of-dopamine-habit-formation-talia-lerner%20.html.

Chapter 12
1. Lane Adams, *How Come It's Taking Me So Long to Get Better?* (Carol Stream, IL: Tyndale House, 1975), 76.

ABOUT THE
AUTHOR

Kirby Kelly is a speaker, influencer, and host of the Bought + Beloved podcast. She has been creating Christian content for over a decade on a multitude of platforms and holds a Masters in Theology from Dallas Baptist University. She and her husband, Richard, live in Dallas, TX, and together they equip ministries with creative media strategies and create engaging content to reach the masses with the joy, truth, and message of the gospel on her platforms. You can connect with her via her website, kirby-kelly.com, or via TikTok, YouTube, or Instagram @KirbyIsABoss.